Catherine, *Her Book*

Also by John Wheatcroft:

DEATH OF A CLOWN, poetry
PRODIGAL SON, poetry
OFOTI, a play
EDIE TELLS, a novel
A VOICE FROM THE HUMP, poetry
A FOURTEENTH-CENTURY POET'S VISION OF CHRIST,
    a poetic drama for voices and instruments
ORDERING DEMONS, poetry

Catherine,
Her Book

John Wheatcroft

New York ● *Cornwall Books* ● *London*

Cornwall Books
440 Forsgate Drive
Cranbury, New Jersey 08512

Cornwall Books
25 Sicilian Avenue
London, WC1A 2QH, England

Cornwall Books
2133 Royal Windsor Drive
Unit 1
Mississauga, Ontario,
L5J 1K5, Canada

Library of Congress Cataloging in Publication Data
Wheatcroft, John, 1925–
  Catherine, her book.

  I. Title.
  PS3573.H4C3   1983   813'.54   81-66295
  ISBN 0-8453-4742-X

Second Printing March 1984

Printed in the United States of America

The conflict is not a rift as a mere cleft is ripped open; rather, it is the intimacy with which opponents belong to each other.

—Martin Heidegger

Bucknell University generously provided the author with opportunity to work on this novel. The Virginia Center for the Creative Arts at Sweet Briar hospitably provided a quiet place. The author wishes to express his gratitude to both.

AUGUST 1, 1783

I'm suffocating.

Everything a wife might ask I've been given. Often he will try to read my wish, then will fulfill what he imagines it to be. As in having me return from the kirk on our wedding day to discover Nelly already implanted in this place as housekeeper. Or in fashioning the new garden, rows of symmetrically laid-out beds of domesticated flowers, canna, gladiolus, iris, brocaded with box. Or in installing the parian mantelpiece and the silver girandoles between the windows in the boudoir next to the drawing room.

Considerately he allows all the freedom and provides all the space I can physically use. I have the grounds. The pony and pony cart and phaeton are at my disposal. I possess this little room or closet, a library exclusively my own.

He's generous, lavishing gifts on me when there's no occasion: books, gowns, jewelry frequently arrive from as far away as London. He has relieved me of all household duties and obligations: Nelly instructs the cook and manages the servants, and he directs the gardener and keeps all accounts himself. Every way is made smooth.

On me he imposes no demand, as I know many men, even gentlemen, do on their wives. He's more than thoughtful and kind. Sensitive to my moods, sympathetic toward my malaise and ennui, indulgent of my occasional fits of temper, he never finds fault or reproaches, he asks no questions. Indeed, he remains gentle, pleasant, even cheerful when I provoke him not to be.

That he much admires me is manifest, although he's too well-bred ever to put me on display. Honoring my disinclination for society, he rarely accepts or extends an invitation. When shortly after our marriage I informed him, without offering explanation, that I should no longer appear in the kirk, he made no inquiry of me, presented no opposition, did not urge contrariwise; indeed, he prevented—I am certain he did—the rector of the parish from seeking out the strayed sheep, as was his pastoral obligation. While he himself continues to attend service faithfully and, I am confident, dutifully reads Scripture and says his prayers in private each day, he instantly discontinued household worship. Although he bows his head for a few seconds of silence before food, he speaks no blessing, and he utters no thanks aloud after eating. All these restraints on himself he practices because he senses how repugnant such forms and exercises have become to me.

I am not so deranged that I fail to recognize his goodness, charity, forbearance, solicitude, and tenderness. Nor am I so depraved that I cannot value his saintlike qualities and conduct. I still remain enough of a moral being to feel gratitude. And I retain sufficient control over my behavior to manifest my respect, whatever black fits, desperations, or wild longings periodically may seize me. I take pains to see that my tantrums and rages never are directed at him. So I satisfy my conscience, conceding that though I fall short of his beatitude, I honestly do my utmost to safeguard his sanity and peace and to preserve his dignity. Marital rectitude is the least I can return him.

Truly I have regard for him. But I'm being smothered.

———————

Disquieting dreams. Not nightmares full of terror like those I sometimes experienced as a child. Dreams, rather, disturbing in the vividness with which personages and events from my girlhood are relived. Although upon my awakening the particularities have gone—and struggle as I do I find it impossible to recall them—I come into consciousness feeling a sense of real presences and actual occurrences, a sense that "they" are nearby or that "it" has just stopped happening. So agitating is this mixture of vagueness and certitude that sometimes of a morning it will take me hours to settle with myself where

[12]

I am, when it is, who is here, what is transpiring. At those times I fear I'm on the verge of lunacy as well as of asphyxiation.

Often I will stay upstairs in the bedroom though I am fully dressed, sitting in the blue great-chair, staring out the window toward the moors for hours, refusing to touch the tea and food Nelly brings, my only occupation being the twisting of the long silver chain of the cairngorm necklace I wear, wrapping and tightening it around my fingers as if trying to strangle them. Often they hurt afterward. Anyone coming upon me surely would imagine I was a devoted papist working at my beads.

AUGUST 10, 1783, AFTERNOON

I've come to a resolution. Or at least I've decided upon a step to be taken. Aware that because of the pain engendered by some great loss, the loss of something which I desperately want, yes, need if I'm to go on breathing in sanity, but which I've hidden from myself in a crevice at the very bottom of my mind, I allowed myself to do what I've forbidden myself since almost six months ago I entered this hall as wife and mistress.

Standing in this closet, or little library, off my husband's and my bedroom, a closet to which I alone have a key—there's not one even in Nelly's bunch—and into which I admit no one, not even my husband, is a small black trunk with a curved lid carved with branches and vines, bound with iron hoops, with iron handles on its ends. As I stared at it this morning after awakening from one of those perturbing dreams and while continuing in a state of frightening muddle, suddenly I remembered that that chest had stood on the wall opposite the large black press in my old bedroom at Wuthering Heights. I determined to open it. It was unlocked. As I lifted the lid the hinges groaned.

On top I found some musty old-fashioned clothing—a girl's

black mourning frock and chemisette, black leather gloves, a pair of ankle-high black suede shoes that laced up the side, a simple black bonnet, a black mantel, and a black petticoat. Delving deeper, I came upon a large inlaid box, which when opened proved to contain: an anatomical drawing of the human body; a wooden soldier, about eight inches high, in a scarlet uniform, rather faded but not peeling, with a white bandoleer; a fruit knife, whose serrated blades folded back into a pearl handle; a tin trumpet; and a half of a walnut shell, carved into the shape of a human skull. As I handled each of these objects, removing, then laying them aside, I felt a series of little starts and quickenings. Spurred on, I finally lifted from the floor of the trunk a maple writing-desk, with a well, caked with dried ink, in the upper lefthand corner and a ledge for quills along the top, to which the lid was hinged.

As I prepared to open the desk, a surge of joy which, though tinged with apprehension, was the most pleasurable sensation I had experienced for a very long time, filled every corner of my being. It was as if I had climbed to the edge of a high promontory and were about to glimpse a wildly beautiful chasm. Indeed, I began to grow dizzy from the height of my anticipation.

AUGUST 10, 1783, EVENING

There they were. Four of them. Smelling of mildew and mold. On top of them lay half a dozen sharp quills. Setting the quills aside I put my fingers on the nearest book. The leather of the binding was dried and cracked. It proved to be an ancient edition of *The Pilgrim's Progress*. Lying beside it, its calfskin cover still soft, was a Testament. On the leather of the two bottom books were embossed letters of faded scarlet: *The Helmet of Salvation* and *The Broad Way to Destruction*. Though I had no intention of reading any such literature, whatever excited spirit was driving me on compelled me to open Bunyan's book.

I took the first page, across from the marbled inside of the front cover, to be embellished with an intricate black design. Peering at the configuration closely I soon discovered that the lines were letters made into words, minuscule, crabbed, virtually without space between them. Something within me leaped, both frightening and thrilling me. The back of that page, the blank space around the printing on the title page, the back of the title page—all similarly covered.

I thumbed through the text. At first the pages seemed to be crammed with type, edge to edge, top to bottom. Closer inspection, however, revealed that the printer had indeed been generous with his margins on all four sides. The same hand that had desecrated the blank page and the title page had imposed its pot-hook and dung-fork calligraphy on every speck of empty paper. Especially welcome to the second author, quite evidently, had been the tops of pages which commenced chapters and the bottoms which closed them. And fortunately for that determined writer the book had been so gathered that a half dozen blank pages had been left at the end. They were economically used.

Similar tiny hieroglyphs adorned, or defaced, the other three volumes in the same way. So thrifty with space had that writer been that, I concluded, another book, virtually as long as the shortest of the four printed volumes, lay superimposed within.

Putting aside *The Broad Way to Destruction*, the last of the four I inspected, I again took up *The Pilgrim's Progress*, opened the cover, and began to decipher the tiny letters. "Catherine Earnshaw, her book. July 24, 1774. Heathcliff was being punished. . . ." Through my eyes the letters H. E. A. T. H. C. L. I. F. F. hit my brain with the force of a blow on the skull from an iron poker. For a split second all of the loose pieces hidden in the pocket of my mind seemed to rattle around loose, like dried beans in a bladder a child is shaking furiously. I may have screamed. It seemed then that the fierce north wind that strips the timber trees of leaves in October and swirls them out of this park in which we are situated, to disperse on the moor sides or fall into becks and brooks, were raging inside my head. Of a sudden the wind stopped. All within was still. I experienced a great peace.

Carrying the now precious volume, I walked back into the bedroom, unhapsed the window, opened it wide, and secured it. A gentle breeze washed across my face; on my skin it felt like a caress made by the very tips of fingers. Riding the breeze was the fragrance of new-mown hay. I drank it in. Easily, freely. It was as if I had just had the sense to remove my head from inside a pillow or bolster in which I had cut a hole and perversely hidden my face.

Sitting in the great-chair beside the open lattice, feeling and drinking in the sweet-scented air, filling myself with its living presence, I recommenced reading those tiny hieroglyphics I had written. I, I knew, was that Catherine Earnshaw.

AUGUST 11, 1783

Outside I preserve my calm detachment. I'm at a fever pitch within. The wild greed, the frenzy with which I'm compelled to devour is shortening my breath again, making me gasp. I think I'll go mad with delirium.

Still I'm enough in control to have adopted a strategy for dealing with the rush of returning life that is threatening to carry me off. The reduced size and extreme crowding of the letters, and the necessity for turning the book from north to east to south to west on each page in order to follow the narrative around the margin, are inhibiting. Yet I'm driven to read so fast that the part of me that experiences again those long-hidden days keeps falling behind the words. I'm determined to sit in this chair beside the open window each morning, afternoon, and evening, as far into late summer and autumn as it takes, with my old writing-desk on my lap, transcribing in the careful hand I now have the leisure to write, making large strokes of and spacing generously, as a limitless supply of fresh sheets allows me, the crabbed letters the Catherine Earnshaw I then was set down, sometimes in racking pain, sometimes in fierce joy. The necessity of writing will pace my consumption. I'll savor, absorb. It will be as if my mind were a blank book in which I'll be reengraving the history of the self I had lost and momently am retrieving.

Kenneth, the doctor, orders me to be sedentary—no riding, even in the phaeton, as little walking as possible. Beside my needle and reading, what else have I to do? My indisposition might be fortuitous, it might provide me the occasion to recover myself.

AUGUST 13, 1783

Glancing ahead at the dates of the entries, I see that Catherine Earnshaw kept her journal in very desultory fashion. Yet the entries in the four books form a continuous narrative. There are a number of extensive accounts of events at a particular time in her life. Then the story will leap ahead—days, months, even years. I wonder what sense such a sporadic recording of a life will make.

I've determined to take still another step. This one quite drastic. Yet not inconsistent with all that I've resolved and done to this point. Nor will it, I hope, distort or in any way corrupt what I am so urgent to recover in its fullness, nor violate the truth of its persisting spirit. We shall see. I can always desist and recommence word-for-word transcription. I know for a surety, however, that if I am to fully recapture the lost life of Catherine Earnshaw, I must do more than impatiently read her cramped and twisting scrawl.

The consideration which thrusts me forward is that when she, or I, commenced the journal, Catherine Earnshaw was but nine years old. It is understandable, therefore, that her childish style was incapable of capturing completely the experience she was driven to record, was too deficient to do justice to her perceptions and emotions, which, though those of a child, were nonetheless acute and intense. Somehow as I read her book, in order to rerecord in an ample plain hand, the

[17]

larger experience and the whole range of thought and depth of feeling retranspire vividly in my mind. The reason this fleshing out, so to speak, occurs, I realize, is that I am indeed not only the scribe and the reader: I am she to whom it happened and in whose mind and memory it lies, recoverable, as the earliest writing on a palimpsest has sometimes proved susceptible to deciphering. The reading and the rerecording of the words are acting as do certain chemicals in bringing forth lines and even colors that have been transcribed invisibly on metal or stone.

Although I commenced proceeding word for word, I soon discovered that the flood of experience the trickle of ink from my pen engendered so took possession of me that I was dissatisfied with the unsophisticated narration of the nine-year-old Catherine. Indeed, it seemed to me that in copying out her literal words I was being not only unfair to *her* because of her limited literary abilities, but untrue to her *life*, which, young as she was, was profound. Since her words did effectively serve to make me relive in mind the whole of what had been, I concluded that finding and setting down, insofar as possible, the words to create or recreate the fullness of experience was the proper way in which to make this strange but life-giving journey of return.

Doing so will take time. That I have aplenty. Immense effort will be called for. That I am willing, yes, am compelled to make. The difficulty, indeed, the impossibility of recapturing the subtleties and the extremities will be discouraging. With myself I have agreed that I must tolerate not only limited success but a certain measure of failure.

Even though my unalterable determination is that no other eye shall ever see this chronicle I have made of Catherine Earnshaw's journal, it must be recorded that I have undertaken and carried on this larger, and I do hope, truer narrative solely for my own sake, to bring a spirit barely existing, a spirit on the brink of extinction back to life, yes, into eternal life.

In executing what I have resolved upon, my hand, I well realize, will have to inscribe words that no Christian woman, let alone the wife of a pious northern gentleman, is expected even to think to herself. To utter such language or to write it down is beyond blasphemy. Perhaps I'll be struck dead in the act. So be it.

Still, the words are not the deed. The words I must transcribe are no more, nor less if they are precise, than the mind's way of acknowledging what already has happened, in this instance deeds committed in whatever of innocence may continue with us from our preincarnate purity into childhood, deeds done out of the freedom of ignorance, yet deeds so dark and terrible that I must wonder those of whose enactment they were were not struck blind, were not turned dumb, were not visited by fire from Heaven or bolts from Hell.

Even as I write, subtle hypocrite that I am, I am compelled to confess that what I have just set down as self-justification is not the whole of the case. It *is* the deed worded in the heart that, happening before the act, makes the act possible. And it *is* the deed worded in the mind that, happening again after the act, keeps the act alive. Thus the deed may be committed times without number in heart and mind, where our moral sovereign sits. In short, the word enables. "For by thy words thou shalt be justified, and by thy words thou shalt be condemned."

This Scripture constitutes the whole article of my belief.

Having destroyed the half dozen sheets of literal transcription I had completed before entering upon my resolution to recreate in its full flesh the life of Catherine Earnshaw, I have determined that tomorrow morning, the fourteenth day of August in the seventeen hundredth and eighty-third year of our Lord, which is the eighteenth year of my existence, I shall begin. I've endured a long season of gloom, misery, and forgetting. Before that there was agony.

[1]
The Pilgrim's Progress

JULY 24, 1774

Heathcliff was being punished by Joseph. For defying the curate. With my father leading cattle to market at K——, Heathcliff and I had planned to spend the day on the moors, the top of Penistone Crags being our particular destination. My father would return for a late supper, I heard him tell Nelly during breakfast, after dark. Gladly we would let Hindley, Nelly, and Joseph have dinner and tea by themselves.

But first it was lesson and catechism with the curate. He arrived before my father left or we'd have sped off. Though I hate to see my father's face cloud when Heathcliff and I disobey. It's not anger exactly. He doesn't scold, as my mother used to. Even when she'd fly up, as she did constantly at Heathcliff, we never paid her mind. She was too feeble to come at us. Then she'd lash out at my father because he wouldn't whip Heathcliff and separate him from me. She'd plain that beggarly Heathcliff was a curse on the house and would prove my ruin. Now Nelly chides us, but only when my father's out of earshot. She rants on about how Heathcliff and I need a firm hand. Mostly she carps at me. I can tell she prefers Heathcliff. Less than Hindley's age, she seems older. Despite that she eats with us, she's a servant. So I don't have to heed her.

The cloud on my father's face is sadness. To behold it

makes me miserable. As if we were on the moors in sunshine, then suddenly the whole top of the world went dark.

Sometimes I notice a gathering of pain on my father's face even when Heathcliff and I have done nothing to vex him. When he's just sitting in the chimney corner beside a lamp with a book on his lap, looking at Heathcliff and me as we lie on a sheepskin thrown on the white stone floor in front of the hearth, sorting feathers we've collected. That's the worst look of all. His brow furrows and his eyes narrow and the dark spot in the bottom of his left irid seems to turn black and he pinches his lips together. As if he were a child trying not to cry. When that look comes over him, something squeezes my insides till I can hardly bear it. And I feel tears come, but I won't ever let them fall when there's somebody there to see. I'll never even let Heathcliff see my cry.

The cloud of sadness is bad enough. I told Heathcliff once how wretched seeing it made me. It didn't him, he said. But when I explained that I hated to feel that way and asked him if we might always mind my father, he agreed. For my sake, he said, not for his. And we've tried. So now usually I see my father's face cloud with sadness only when Hindley or Nelly or Joseph or the curate tells on us. We'll never pay them mind.

So when the curate arrived this morning and my father called, Heathcliff and I came running into the sitting room from the back kitchen, where we'd been regimenting the wooden soldiers, using the seat of the settle for a battlefield. While the curate heard us our geography, my father sat beside the window with a book. I could tell that he was only pretending to read.

I knew the lesson pretty well. It was British rivers. The only one the curate asked me that I couldn't locate was the Usk. I guessed it ran through Devon.

"Wrong. Think again, Miss Catherine," the curate said, tapping his forehead with two fingers. "Recollect properly. The Usk." Greasehorn that he was, he kept glancing at my father.

With a couple of quick strokes Heathcliff chalked an unmistakable figure of a whale on his slate. It had a huge tail and he placed a little round eye in the top of its head. After it he drew an S. But I was too proud to give his answer as my own. When the curate turned to him, he pretended not to know.

"Very good, on the whole, Miss Catherine, quite commendable," the curate simpered, nodding his head. It was clear he was fawning before my father. Then he turned to Heathcliff. Heathcliff despises the curate. As much for his ignorance as for his foppishness. As he rattled off the names of rivers and Heathcliff provided wrong answers, although he knew almost all of them, I'm certain, we could see that the curate a number of times had to check himself in his book. Heathcliff put rivers in the most absurd places—the Cam in Oxford, for example, and the Ouse in Cornwall. I watched the curate's wafer-colored cheeks flush with anger. Too stupid to realize that Heathcliff was mocking him, he took it as an affront that his pupil had not learned his lesson.

"Now, Mr. Heathcliff," he would chide, with one eye on my father, "mental sloth, we must remember, also is a sin." Or some such flummery. Observing his left fist clenched on the side of his chair away from my father, I knew that only my father's presence restrained him from giving Heathcliff a box on the ear.

That had been the curate's way with Heathcliff almost from the time he first came for lessons, after my mother died. My mother had taught us only our hornbook and numbers. Two days ago when the curate, who had us pent in the sitting room with himself alone, drove his fist into the side of Heathcliff's head and called him a dunderpate for putting Richard the Second early in the century and Edward the Second at the end, I saw lightning flash in Heathcliff's eyes, and Heathcliff's own fists clenched as he went leaping out of further reach. I doubt the curate noticed. Or if he did, I judged him too little aware of Heathcliff's temper, too trusting to his own age and position to be able to imagine receiving a physical reply.

"I'll not endure one more touch of his cowardly finger," Heathcliff had declared to me afterward, as we lay in the straw in the loft of the cowbarn, listening to Joseph bawling

Heathcliff's name throughout the farmyard. Then we went on to see who could imagine the most ingenious torture machine. Mine was superior, Heathcliff agreed, because his depended upon blades and teeth, which would quickly draw blood and thus lead to the release of the victim into early death, whereas my contraption was an arrangement of well-situated screws, as in a cider press.

Excusing himself to the curate and bidding us be good children, my father took up his hat and walking stick, and departed. I thought I detected a look of cumber on his face. That gave me an instant of pain. Then it passed.

"Now, my man," the curate began in a fleering tone the second the door scrooped closed behind my father, "we'll see whether you've been attending to the lesson our Lord enjoined you to learn any more diligently than you've mastered the lesson your earthly mentor assigned." Whereupon, heedless of me, he assaulted Heathcliff with a barrage of questions on minute points of Old Testament Scripture. Watching him out of slightly narrowed eyes, Heathcliff sat with his lips compressed so tightly they might have been sealed.

"But, Mr. Shielders," I interposed, hoping to prevent what I feared was coming because it would surely threaten Heathcliff's and my plan to spend the rest of the day on the moors, "yesterday you charged us to study the fifth chapter of St. Matthew and to commit to memory verses three through twelve. And I dare say Heathcliff has done so, for he recited all eight Beatitudes without mistake while we were collecting eggs for Nelly before breakfast."

"I'll thank you to allow me to conduct catechism in my own way, Miss," the curate responded, barely able to use civil words to me because I dared defend Heathcliff. To be sure, I did not reveal that in reciting the Beatitudes Heathcliff had cast them all in the negative. "The questions I am putting are such that any decent Christian ought to be able to answer at any time. Well," he demanded, turning back to Heathcliff, "what have you to say in defense of your heathen ignorance?"

Returning the curate's glare, Heathcliff kept his eyes steadily on him, marking him as a farm dog might watch an intruding lapdog who does not know he's being measured for attack. Heathcliff, I've noticed, for some reason blinks much less frequently than do most human beings. The curate's face, on the other hand, fat and jowly, though he's but a few years older than Hindley, is full of cheek twitches and he is forever swallowing—his own saliva, I suppose—and his eyelids flutter like moth wings.

All at once, unable any longer to bear Heathcliff's stare of defiance, the curate leaped from his chair and with both fists clenched rushed toward where Heathcliff was sitting on the side of the hearth opposite me. Heathcliff's steady gaze had been as vigilant as it was contemptuous. The instant the curate moved, Heathcliff sprang to his feet. And by the time the curate had reached him, he had snatched the poker from where it stood next to the bellows. With his right arm upraised, the poker grasped in his hand, Heathcliff stood not too many inches beneath the curate, who stopped short on his toes and stared. Protruding from his smock, Heathcliff's bare arm looked sinewy. I imagined the curate's under his coat to be as flabby as his cheeks. Fire was burning in Heathcliff's black eyes.

"You would, would you, you young devil!" the curate gasped.

Heathcliff, never moving a muscle, seeming scarce to breathe, let the holding of his posture bear his reply. Drained of the flash of self-indulgent anger, the curate's face had turned tallowy. I could tell he was weighing whatever little courage he possessed against Heathcliff's young strength and obvious determination. His fortitude, proving to be a hollow counter of tin rather than a measure of iron, flew up in the scale.

"Help!" he shrieked. "Help! Heathcliff is attacking me with the poker." To think of such a man ascended on Sunday above the heads of the congregation and reading in that reedy voice of his the Psalm about the Lord of Hosts, the Lord mighty in battle, disgusted me. Even when he shouted in fear the sound seemed to issue from his narrow humped nose.

Just then I heard the rattle of a cart as it rolled up the rutty lane. Joseph, as ill luck would have it. Taking heart at the noise, the curate bawled again. Heathcliff, also hearing the cart and knowing that the might of Joseph's huge arm equaled the severity of his judgment and his readiness for punishment, dropped the poker. It clanged to the stones beside the coal scuttle. Darting into the back kitchen, Heathcliff ran into the embrace of Joseph as he entered, like a woodcock into a springe clap-net.

To no avail I contradicted the curate's lying assertion that Heathcliff had swung the poker at his head and, missing, had flung it at him as he fled. Nor did my threat to appeal to my father upon his return for strict justice to Heathcliff and retribution on his wrongdoers, of whom I declared Joseph should constitute one if he attempted to mete out punishment, carry any force. I shouted for Nelly in order to secure her as ally and witness, knowing her partiality to Heathcliff, but she had left the house and, presumably, the farmyard.

There was no help for it. At best Heathcliff's and my plan for an all-day excursion on the moors would have to be revised to our disadvantage. For, muttering through clenched teeth as he worked his lantern jaw like a cow's about the vengeance of the Lord against the Philistines and the Hittites and the Amalekites, Joseph joggled Heathcliff off by the collar of his smock to work out his "flaysome disobedience" by laboring at his side for the rest of the day—replacing slates on the roof of the cow barn. To himself he chortled that sparing the hand whom he had been planning to commandeer to assist him, for work in the field with the rest of the men would be thrift. Our only consolation was that Hindley also was off somewhere. Had he been present for the altercation, he would have seen to it that Heathcliff not escape a flogging. And with the double warding he would have provided, Heathcliff would have had little chance to slip the collar.

His cowardice exposed to himself, Heathcliff, and me, the curate, after glancing at his pinchbeck watch, was glad enough to don his shovel hat, then go slinking out the front door toward Gimmerton at the earliest opportunity. Leaving through the back door an instant later, I set off in the opposite direction, toward the moors. As I passed Heathcliff in the yard, unloading slates from the cart in relay with Joseph, I understood from the quick nod of his head, first toward me, then toward the path leading to Penistone Crags, that I was to go on and wait for him there. And from his glance at the ladder inside the barton, leant against the stone side of the byre, I was assured that he would take his leave and join me as soon as either he or Joseph climbed to the roof. Were it Heathcliff who ascended, I imagined he would simply scrabble up over the gable, steep as it was, then leap from the edge of the roof on the other side into the stack of first-cut hay that was waiting to be pitched into the barn. Were Joseph to climb to the roof, Heathcliff, I knew, would remove the ladder and speed off.

Joseph, it turned out, made the mistake of climbing. Even as I write this journal at the end of this curious day, a day as unsettled as the weather on the moors can be, bright and gloomy and weird in its light by turns, I laugh to think of Joseph bawling Heathcliff's name, demanding that Jehovah avenge His servant and punish the plisky sinner, praying for Jacob's ladder, I suppose, to provide him a means of descent. Joseph was too fond of his old bones, I have no doubt, to risk them clambering up over the gable, then pitching them into a rick of hay.

Because they were stacking wheat in a croft on the other side of the rise behind the barn, none of the field hands heard his prayers and imprecations. So he had ample time for both. Nor did Nelly or Hindley return to rescue him. Not until the dairy maid came back in midafternoon was a ladder provided for his descent. I am anxious to behold him in the morning, for he never came to supper nor sat in the living room reading his Bible, as is his wont, but spent the whole of the evening in his garret bedroom. I hope the sun has him looking as if he'd been fried in Hell.

———————

Out on the moor, even on top of the swells, the sky seemed ever so far away. Blue above, except where the sun made a

[26]

golden hole. Along the highest rises, some woolly clouds. And a few little floating islands of fleece.

Though it was warm, wind whistled in my ears. Every so often it would die and I could hear the cry of a bird, a lapwing or moorcock, and the gurgle of becks still running hard from yesterday's rain. Loosestrife, thistle, harebell, and foxglove were blooming on the lower slopes. Higher up, the first pink of the heather was brightening the blackish green of its foliage among the brighter green of the bracken.

A bird perched on top of the dead tree trunk, where the path veers off toward Gimmerton down the valley. Rising above the bent as it does, without any limbs, solitary, hard, as if turning to stone, it reminds me, I once told Heathcliff, of Lot's wife after she was changed to a pillar of salt on the plain of Zoar. He said to him it looked like the statue of Baal, Ahab was punished for worshiping in Samaria. Before I was close enough to distinguish the bird it took wing. From the way it hung in the wind I guessed it was a kestrel.

When I reached the guidepost, a tapering four-sided stone which, rearing upright, stood taller than I, marking where the path that leads from Gimmerton to Thrushcross Grange meets the path that leads from our house to Penistone Crags, I ran my fingers in the grooved letters carved into the four sides, G, TG, WH, PC, as I always do. I like the gritty feel. And then I knelt and delved into the hole in the soil at the base. Heathcliff had discovered it. One day, when we had reached in deeper than we could see, overcoming our fear of a snake or a lizard, we found a hoard of spiraling snail shells and prettily colored stones—ruby and emerald and turquoise. I imagined they were gems a pirate had hidden there just before he was taken and hanged. But Heathcliff insisted they were only pebbles that you can find in the bed of a brook under a waterfall. When I asked who had put them there, he answered, "A witch." Almost surely, we both knew, it had been Hindley and Nelly years before.

Later we added some treasure of our own: A drawing of a naked body, with red and blue lines thickly circuiting it,

[27]

which we tore from a mildewed book we found in the garrett one rainy Sunday. The way it's drawn between the legs you can't tell whether it's a man or a woman. A little tin trumpet my father once brought Hindley as a present when he returned from a trip to B ____. It really plays. Heathcliff took it from Hindley's room one day after Hindley had beaten him, and was planning to melt it in a fire he made inside a circle of stones behind the wash-house. But I said that was a stupid way of getting revenge, destroying rather than possessing the thing you took. Heathcliff answered that he couldn't bear to own anything that had Hindley's touch on it. So we hid the trumpet here. A half a walnut shell Heathcliff had carved into the shape of a skull. At first he told me that he had found it in the fairy cave under Penistone Crags and that it was the skull of one of the little brown creatures that make green rings and that Joseph leaves morsels of cake and cheese for on the kitchen table every Christmas Eve. We kept it hid in a lacquer box in our room, but when I started to have nightmares about it that made me scream and wake Heathcliff, he told me the truth. Even though I believed him, I insisted it be removed from our room. So we hid it here. A pearl-handled fruit knife with serrated blades that fold back into the case. My father brought this as a present for me the time he brought Hindley the tin trumpet. Before Heathcliff and I hid it here, I used the point of the larger blade to scratch CATHERINE EARNSHAW into the paint on the ledge of the casement window beside my cabinet bed. And one of our wooden soldiers, reluctant as we were to give him up, so that there would be someone to guard the treasure. Everything was intact.

As I followed the path toward the head of the valley, the swells rising more steeply on either hand, I felt like an Israelite crossing through the parting of the Red Sea. The white bodies of the grazing moor sheep looked like spots of foam. Here there was less wind, and the gill that paralleled the path, although concealed by the low ridge that runs down the valley like a knobby spine, gurgled as it rushed toward the falls. Frequently I glanced behind me to see whether Heathcliff was coming, although remembering the load of slate on the wagon

I doubted that he'd be able to escape the reach of Joseph's long arm for yet a while.

Arriving at the place where the path divides again, the lower track following the ridge and the gill and the splash, finally to take you along the bottom of the force to the foot of the crags, the other curving off to the north and climbing the rise toward the top of the crags, I could hear the crash of the falls ahead on the lower path. This sound gave me the feeling that the dark green walls of the sea were indeed rushing back together and that I, now a pursuing Egyptian footman, mommently would be drowned. Although it would mean a longer wait up there for Heathcliff, I quickened my step. The game of crossing the Red Sea had become a bit frightening, like some of my dreams. Were Heathcliff with me, playing the game, too, and were I to tell him my fear, he'd scoff at it, I knew, without scorning me. Thinking about Heathcliff afforded me courage. That I knew I should need for what lay ahead.

Although I had been glad that Heathcliff and I had made our plan to climb to the top of the crags today, now I wished more than ever that he were with me. Most often we follow the gill past the water-splash leading to the force, where the two sides of the valley almost touch, and cross the scree to the fairy cave under the crags, directly in front of which, beside the pool, is a patch of bright yellow sand, gold dust, we call it. Using the cave we play at games like Jonah and the whale, Daniel and the lions, Joseph in the pit, and Lazarus come forth. The last time we were there Heathcliff made up a new game out of *The Pilgrim's Progress*—the cave was set in the hill of Lucre, he was Demas, and I was Christian. It didn't turn out as it does in Bunyan's book. Heathcliff can think up the most exciting ways for us to do stories together. We never play them the same way twice. Sometimes when I think of something to add, Heathcliff will say it's stupid and we won't do it. Then I want to cry, but I never do. Sometimes, though, he'll say I'm canny and we'll do what I think of. I feel proud then but I never let him know it.

Our plan today had been to follow the path up the rise to

where it ends as the rocks begin, then to climb over the boulders toward the farthest jut at the very edge of the cliff. The
jut is narrow, and you're so high up your breath goes and
when you look out into the gorge you feel dizzy. The last time
we took this path and climbed to the top of the crags, we tried
to crawl to the very end of the jut, something we'd never
dared. Halfway out I couldn't get my breath and my head was
spinning so that I was unable to go any farther. But Heathcliff
on his hands and knees scrambled all the way to the edge. I
was terrified he'd fall.

When he returned to where on the rock I'd retreated after
backing off the jut, he didn't make fun of me or chide me for
my fear. He never does.

From where we were then sitting on the rocks and from as
far as I had dared crawl on the jut, you can see the gill as it
rushes toward the falls where the ridge gives way, and you can
see some of the den and well into the gorge. But from the very
end of the jut, Heathcliff told me, you can see the scree and
that patch of golden sand at the bottom and, if you lean over,
even the mouth of the fairy cave. Then I remembered looking
up at the crags from below and seeing that the jut so protrudes
that it overhangs the sheer face of the cliff.

After he'd told me about what he had seen, I promised
Heathcliff that the next time we came I'd venture all the way
out to the edge and look over, as he had done. Today was that
day.

As I climbed up the rise where it crosses the wold, before
the steeper ascent to the rocks, the wind increased. Again it
was whistling in my ears, drowning out the roar of the force,
which I was bending away from. No longer was I crossing the
Red Sea with the threat of being swallowed up. Now I was
Moses climbing Mount Nebo, to the top of Pisgah, for a
glimpse of the Promised Land. Suddenly I sensed rather than
heard a living being behind me. Wheeling, I saw it was only a
moor sheep wandered off from the flock that grazed the lower
bank of the wold, which was green with the more plentiful
grass, onto the path. With its black face raised it stared after me.

The upper reach of the wold, which I had now attained,

was high enough to grant me a view of the path all the way past the guidepost and the dead tree trunk. They rose from the low nabs they occupied like upright thumbs from giant fists. No Heathcliff.

Then the gray and black earth, in which grew bracken and ling, began turning mahogany, the color of the skin of an Indian prince. Glancing ahead, I could see the highest rocks of Penistone shining golden under the midday sun. How different that stone from the dark gray and black that studs the moors and is set into walls which wind every which way across the sides of the dales, like dark chains binding the body of a prostrate Gulliver, and are reared into farm houses, barns, and outbuildings clustered here and there on the moorland!

As I arrived at the first part of the cliff and began climbing the boulders, I sensed how close to the earth the sky had come. Almost it seemed I could reach out and seize a handful of fleece or by stretching my arms could take the sun, which now was not a hole but a yellow ball, in my hands and draw it to me and send it rolling down the path behind me to knock over the guidepost and the tree trunk. Although the ascent was steep, I didn't taste a spice of fear until I gained the top, where, squatting on what formed a stone platform, I could see the drop-off beyond the edge. And now, even though up here the wind was blasting my ears, through it or in it I was able to pick up the crash of the water I saw rushing over the lip of the falls to go splashing onto the rocks in the gorge below. Ahead—that jut I had to dare. I removed my boots and stockings.

Throwing one last look behind me across the whole sweep of the vale and seeing no moving speck that might be Heathcliff, I dropped onto my hands and knees as I reached the spot where the cliff narrows like a pair of shoulders and the neck begins. Against my bare knees, for my skirts were pushed up, and the palms of my hands, the stone was rough, sharp-edged at times. Glancing ahead, close to the rock as I was, all I could see was blue sky. I seemed to be suspended in it. I looked neither right nor left.

Now I had moved myself out on the jut, farther than I had

dared to go before. Breathing again was becoming difficult, quick and short sucks I took, and I felt light-headed and dizzy. To imagine telling Heathcliff when he arrived, then to do it again with him without hesitation and to see him eye me not with envy but with approval, yes, admiration, though he would never permit a trace of a smile to show, let alone give praise words—the desire for such a joyful moment kept me going. Fearful the wind, which was buffeting me from the left, might huff me over the edge to the right, I dropped from my hands and knees onto my belly. Drawing deep breaths, I lay for a while without moving. Suddenly I seemed to turn light as air, my flesh felt weightless. So as not to go sailing upward in the blue toward the sun, I pressed the length of my body hard against the rock, seized two ridges I found with my fingers, tried to curl my toes so they might take hold of something solid. That helped.

Now I stared at the stone directly beneath me. It sparkled in the sunlight. Where my forehead would touch were I to kiss the rock, a Z-shaped streak flashed, as if lightning were buried in the cliff. Then, like a cautious snake, I slithered slowly forward on my belly. Now I was close enough to the edge for my raised eyes to see, beyond the top of the jut, the lower, sloping wold across the chasm. The moor sheep grazing in that high meadow looked like tombstones on a green sward. Through my apron and frock and petticoat I could feel the jags and ridges of the stone scraping my body. The wind was a howl and a shove. As the fingers of my right hand, sliding ahead, curled over the end of the jut, I gasped. The stone felt pummy-smooth. There I was.

I rested. Raising my eyes without lifting my face, I looked straight ahead. The tops of the hills across the gorge, from which the bank of clouds had disappeared, seemed to be supporting the sky. Allowing the fingers of my right hand still to overlap the tip of the jut, I stretched my left arm out and curled the fingers of that hand also over the edge. Had I eyes in the knobs of my fingers, they would be looking directly down into the funnel-shaped chasm. But my fingers were blind. It had to be with the eyes in my leaning-over head that I

[32]

stared down into the abyss, as had Heathcliff. That was the fulfillment of what I was daring.

Pulling hard on a little rim or ridge that my fingers felt out on the foremost part of the jut, I tugged myself forward, an inch at a time, until my forehead protruded over the brink. Yet my downcast eyes still stared into stone. Three times I shifted forward, wriggling on my belly. As my eyes cleared the end and went over the brink, I smashed them closed.

I sucked for breath in the wind. In the dark my eyelids made, I could feel myself spinning in a whirlpool. Although the air was cool from the blow, I felt myself to be flames as I fell twisting into the narrowing throat of the blackness. Fear tore open my eyes.

It was as Heathcliff had said—the bottom of the gorge seemed almost as far away as the sky. Although all was blurred from the spinning either the world or I was engaged in, still I could make out the water below, bubbling white as it surged through the rapids at the foot of the cataract, then black as a well bottom in the little round pool at the base of the funnel, to go slowly gray-green as it flowed calmly through the high pastures the landscape fell into. And there were the dark rocks around the fringe of the pool, there the bright yellow sand in front of the fairy cave, and there the black mouth of the cave itself. My damp body went cool. I drank in the wind. The spinning slowed and stopped.

Able to bear the height, I resisted an impulse to inch my way backward instantly now that I'd dared see what Heathcliff had. As the whirling ended and the blurring cleared, I began to distinguish rocky slabs and shelves directly beneath me, stunted pine and thorn growing in clefts, their roots naked as they struggled for nourishment in the little deposits of soil, like the bony arms and legs of a heap of dead men twisted together, fringes of tall reddish green reeds poking up among rocks around the inky pool. Now that I was focusing clearly, the bottom of the gorge didn't seem quite so far away as at first it had. And there on the golden sand two large birds, one black, one gray. The birds sat perfectly still.

Suddenly to my surprise a human figure appeared, emerg-

[33]

ing from the mouth of the cave. I thought it might be Heath-cliff. But it was next to impossible he would forget our plan to climb to the top in order to dare the jut together. Then I saw that the person's hair was brown in the sunlight.

Almost instantly a second figure emerged from the cave. It was a woman with long loose-flowing hair, also brown. When neither of the birds flew off, something inside me leaped. The birds were heaps of clothing, the two human forms were naked. The first personage was Hindley; the second, Nelly.

I was unable to remove my eyes from between their legs. From the distance at which I was looking, I could see it was dark there, in contrast to the rest of their bodies—Hindley's a shade darker than Nelly's. My heart thumped.

Hindley and Nelly were standing, up against each other now, sideways to me. All at once Nelly fell to her knees in front of him. A weakness swept over me. I told myself that I must not faint or likely I'd go rolling off the side of the jut or plunge headfirst over the edge. With the fingers of both hands I seized the ridge near the tip of the rock and squeezed with all my might. I couldn't make myself close my eyes again or look away.

Now Hindley's hands, which had been on Nelly's shoulders, clapped themselves onto her titsies, which were not like mine and Heathcliff's and Hindley's, little pink berries, nor even the size of green pears as my mother's had been, but were large as half a muskmelon. Bending his knees, he jiggled them up and down. Nelly had her hands on Hindley's nether cheeks. Suddenly, as if he were a sapling and a furious wind were uprooting him, Hindley lunged forward onto the sand, knocking Nelly over backward so that he landed on top of her. After a few seconds of thrashing together, their bodies rolled apart and lay as if dead, Hindley face-down on the sand, Nelly with her face toward the sky. I couldn't wrench my eyes from the plat of darkness between her legs. Heathcliff and I were not like that.

All of whatever my innards are made of had turned to water, warm water. Though I told myself to keep my fingers clamped on the ridge of the rock and though my body lay

[34]

stretched full-length on the rough hard jut, I could scarcely feel the stone. I wanted to flow. The idea of rushing over the side and dropping like water down the cataract into the pool below now prompted no fear. Not wrinkling them tight as I had before, I let my eyelids fall closed. With my inner eye, in the golden haze of the sun filtering through my lashes and lids, I beheld circles of pure color, pinks and reds and purples, growing out of points until the circles swelled so large they dissolved. Now the wind was a voice, crying and sighing about my head. I lay within a huge warm drop of water. I was gone out of the world. I was the water.

"Cathy, Cathy," the wind was soughing in my ear. Now I could feel again the hard stone against my left side. Turning my head so as not to look down into the chasm when I first reopened my eyes, I beheld Heathcliff's eyes as I raised my lids. They were blacker than the pool below and were steeped with admiration, the admiration that my craving for had driven me to the tip of the crag.

Knowing how narrow the jut, I let go of the ridge of rock I still was clutching and drew Heathcliff against me by clasping my arms around his neck.

"Look, Heathcliff," I murmured, putting my lips against his ear, for the wind was whistling again, "look down there."

Turning his face from me, he peered into the gorge.

"It isn't so high as you fear before you make yourself look," he said. "Have you seen?"

"Yes," I replied. "But that's not what I mean. Look closely. On the sand."

"I am."

"Don't you see them?"

"The moorcock and moorhen, you mean?"

Lifting my face from his cheek and turning my head, I peered into the chasm. Hindley and Nelly were gone. Only two birds stood on the sand. I knew they *were* birds because when Heathcliff rolled a loose pebble from the jut and it dropped through the long air and went splashing into the black pool, making a water spout, they took wing.

I haven't yet told Heathcliff what I saw.

[35]

JULY 25, 1774

Mist. So wet we seemed to be walking through water. The heights of the moors were lost in the sky. Gimmerton Valley was a scoop of cloud. In the lower reaches of the wold only the black faces of the moor sheep were visible at any distance. As if ghosts were gathering, ghosts wearing dark masks. Heathcliff and I were heading for Black Horse Marsh.

Neither Joseph nor the curate had complained of Heathcliff to my father. For different reasons. Both selfish, for they both hated Heathcliff. Joseph because his pride would not let him acknowledge his humiliating defeat. But he'll bide his time and make Heathcliff pay later, beyond any doubt. Not even Hindley can bear a grudge better than Joseph. Not that Heathcliff cares—let Joseph flog him hard as he likes. Heathcliff is too proud to tell. So Joseph knows he can thrash Heathcliff with impunity whenever my father is gone.

The curate had ample opportunity to inform on Heathcliff, for my father stayed in the house this morning, sipping tea while reading beside the chimney piece. (Though he tries to suppress it, my father's cough is bothering him still.) It's clear now that Shielders has come to fear Heathcliff. Besides, he is well aware that Heathcliff would only be admonished, not punished. My father almost never punishes Heathcliff. Yet he severely inflicts punishment on Hindley and me. Often he strikes Hindley. And he constantly disciplines me by depriving me and cribbing me up in my room. Sometimes I think my father hates Hindley, his own son. And I know he prefers Heathcliff to me, his daughter. The realization used to drive me frantic with jealousy, before my mother died. But now I'm so much attached to Heathcliff that I no longer mind. Indeed, we're so close, Heathcliff and I, that it seems my father in loving him as he does also loves me the more. It scarcely works so for Hindley, he and Heathcliff hating each other as they do.

Feigning civility, the curate had us review rivers and mountains as our lesson. Both of us knew everything. Next Heath-

[36]

cliff recited verses three through twelve of the fifth chapter of St. Matthew without a stumble. Then we both listened with an assumed respect as the curate sermonized us on the Beatitudes, although it took all of our willpower to hear him pompously prattle about the poor in spirit and the meek and the merciful and the pure in heart without erupting into laughter. Only my father's presence restrained us. None of the three of us wanted any trouble this morning. The curate, because he's a coward. Heathcliff and I, because we were relieved that yesterday's conflict had not been reported and because we realized that if we endured for a spell we'd be free. So it turned out.

As we were crossing the cowslip lea, where the bull grazes, a fine rain set in. And the wind, which had died overnight, sprang up again. Heathcliff and I wouldn't go to the trouble of skirting that pasture, as everyone except Joseph and the hands do. Even my father. But we did stay close enough to the wall that we might go scrambling up and over should the bull snort and charge us, with his fiery saucer eyes glaring, as he sometimes has.

No sooner did we reach the moor than the slanting, gale-driven rain pierced us to the skin. I could feel the drops sting and prick, like the pointed nails of a witch. Over our blouses we had on only pinafores, Heathcliff without cap, I without bonnet. Although the summit of summer, it was cold as November. I reproached myself for not having thrown the gray frieze cloak of the dairymaid, which hangs on a wooden peg in the milking shed, over my shoulders—silently, for I would never let Heathcliff know that I minded the cold. Truly I didn't care about either wet or wind.

So much rain had fallen all season that the becks almost immediately were full to overflowing. Joseph kept muttering that it was punishment from on high for our errant ways, as in the days of Noah. He was hoping for destruction, I knew, so long as he was spared. My father lamented the loss of a large measure of first hay and the sogginess of the fields for second plowing. Before our eyes Heathcliff and I could see the gullies

[37]

turning into freshets. Soon we were slogging through black mud that clung to our boots and we were forced to ford new-made rindles and runnels in every little clough and down.

Climbing a rise just after we left the path, its upright stones daubed with lime to serve as markers, which winds four miles on to Thrushcross Grange, where the Lintons live, we heard in the wind the jingle of bells. Looking up, for we had had to lower our faces as we'd headed into the stinging rain, we saw approaching, seemingly dropped from the low sky, the dun packhorses of a caravan headed for the mills in K——, in single file, their noses down to their pasterns, their mulelike ears laid back along their skulls, their flanks bulging with haycock-size trussings of wool, as if they were bloated from having drowned and floated in water for days. Their shaggy coats looked wet as swamp moss. To let them pass and to avoid being seen by the two drovers that plodded behind them, carrying switches, as bent and as wet and as shaggy as the animals, Heathcliff and I scrambled out of the narrow gang and crouched behind a big clump of besom.

"They're trying to take food into Jericho," Heathcliff whispered, "and we're spies of Joshua." And we played that game while they passed so close we might have reached through the twigs of the broom and pulled off gobs of wool or tugged on the drenched cloaks of the drovers, who never knew we were there. After the beasts and the men vanished into the rain-filled gloom, the ring of the harness bells being carried away from our ears by the rush of the wind, we kept up the game.

Long before we reached Blackhorse, we were so steeped and muckymucked that we might as well have been wallowing in the marsh. Beneath my pinafore and blouse and skirt and even beneath my drawers and stockings, my skin was as wet as my face and bare arms. After meeting the caravan, we had given up crossing all but the deepest rivulets and bournes on stones and had just gone draggling through mud and sloshing through water that covered our boot tops. We saw only two or three birds, kestrels, who relish the wind.

Arrived at the marsh, we stopped being Joshua's spies and played with the porriwiggles, which exhibited themselves in plenty, stirring their tails with a finger, then darting our hands into the frigid peaty water in order to snatch them. In the blackness of the bog pools they were hard to follow. When you caught one, it felt cold as stone and was slippery as a moist squash seed. After holding it for a while, we'd let it go by opening our fist just enough for it to squeeze with a spring through the slit our first finger made. From a flat stone we found among the rushes, on which we placed our knuckles, we measured the greatest leap by jamming a stick in the mud of the bog where we saw the splash that was larger than the pimples the hard-driving rain made on the skin of the water. One of mine jumped farthest. To feel the tadpole wriggle inside my palm, then go slithering out like a squeezed grape was a pleasing sensation.

When we judged it midafternoon, we headed for home. In order to let ourselves and our clothing dry by teatime, we decided to seclude ourselves in the hayloft of the byre. By the time we reached the farmyard, the wind had died to a gentle breeze, and though the rain still fell, the tops of the moors began to emerge as the sky lifted and brightened. When we passed the horse trough beside the stable, Heathcliff removed his hand from the pocket of his pantaloons. Something squirted from his fist and went splashing with a gurgle into the dark water.

"May it turn to a frog the size of my head and leap into Joseph's churlish face and frighten him as if it were Beelzebub," Heathcliff laughed. "Some day while he's watering the cart horse." No one was in sight as we made our way among the cows in the barton.

Inside the barn, out of the rain and the breeze, everything was still. The darkness thickened as we moved from the door toward the ladder. I had already begun climbing when I heard a rustle above me, something more than the scurry of a rat. I glanced upward. Feet without clogs or boots, and legs without stockings beneath a skirt and petticoat were descending. In order to spare my fingers a stepping on, I unwrapped them from the rung they curved around and went leaping to the earthen floor, packed hard as flagstone from the hoofs of cows.

[39]

Sensing a presence above, Heathcliff had darted behind the big hinged door.

I thought I heard a scroop in the loft overhead.

"Oh, it's you, Nelly," I exclaimed, loud enough for Heathcliff to hear so that he'd know he need not fear Hindley or Joseph.

"Yes, Catherine," she replied, as she stepped onto the floor beside me, "I was searching for eggs. Some of the hens have taken to roosting and laying in the loft."

In the shaft of light the open door allowed to enter, I saw that Nelly carried no basket. Nor was she using a bonnet as a depository for eggs, although she wore no head covering. I noticed wisps of hay caught in her long flowing hair and sticking in her bodice.

"Oh," was all I could utter, echoing myself. For I felt my innards going soft and my brain beginning to whirl in confusion. Midafternoon was indeed a strange time to be collecting eggs.

"You look like a drowned whelp." Nelly's tone changed from that of defendant to that of accuser. "I advise you to get yourself dried out and looking respectable for tea. Your father wouldn't be happy to know you'd been off romping in this rain. The same counsel is meant for Heathcliff. I allow he's skulking somewhere hereabouts, in much the same bedraggled condition."

As soon as Nelly went skifting out of the barn, Heathcliff emerged. Standing together in the shadow just beyond the doorway, we watched her vamp up the causeway of the garden, beneath the pear tree by the wash-house, past Joseph's gooseberry and currant bushes, to disappear into the back kitchen. I wondered whether Heathcliff had observed that she was barefoot. Again I mounted the ladder, Heathcliff behind me.

Light was streaming into the loft, the big square door of which stood open. Through it I could see the huge wooden block with the fall on it that protruded from the eaves of the barn into the yard. Heathcliff and I moved to the opening with one accord. We looked down into the wet stack of hay,

[40]

into which yesterday Heathcliff would have jumped had Joseph sent him to the roof of the barn.

The rain had stopped; not a drop pinged on the slates of the roof. As I breathed the air in, a mingling of the fragrance of the wet moorland turf, the scents rising from the garden, the musty smell of the straw, and the reek of the cows, I felt myself going soft inside again, as if my bones were mud, my flesh water. Even while we watched through the open frame of the door, the gray of the sky came lighter and began to blue and then the late afternoon sun stood revealed, at first a rim of dark apricot, then all rose-tinged gold. Taking Heathcliff by the hand, I pulled him down into the hay spread on the floor of the loft, just to the left of the open door. Although he lay in shadow, I still could see that glorious sun.

The hay was wet.

"Move over here," I said; "the rain has driven in through the open door."

"No, it hasn't," answered Heathcliff. "The wind was carrying the storm from the north and east. That water leaked through the places where the roof is still waiting to be mended." He laughed, so that his teeth glistened in the darkness, and I joined him. "Besides, the door of the loft was closed. I looked up at it as we crossed the barton. Nelly must have opened it before she descended."

I doubted that *Nelly* had opened it. Again that rush of feeling within me. Now that I knew I had indeed seen two heaps of clothing at the foot of Penistone Crags yesterday, that the sight of naked bodies I had seen joined so strangely, then wrestling together on the sand, was no vision of angels or demons, I was ready to tell Heathcliff. I could not have gone on withholding from him.

Scuttling to where the hay was dry, we lay side by each. Now sunlight bathed us both, warmingly. Still wet, his long black curly hair, plastered on his forehead, hung down over his eyes. In the rose-gold light the skin of his face, though swarthy, seemed thin and looked almost translucent. I could see the high bones of his cheeks and the sockets of his cavernous eyes as distinctly outlined as yesterday I had seen the

[41]

curves and hollows and sheer lines of the cliff. Squeezing his hand, I felt his strong fingers and the network of little bones in the top of his palm.

"Heathcliff," I began softly, "would you ever put your tinkler in somebody's mouth?" To speak the word "tinkler" to him took as much courage as it had to edge to the tip of the jut yesterday afternoon.

I felt the slightest tremor in his hand. Around the block, the end of which I could see protruding over the barnyard like a gibbet, a swarm of gnats revolved elliptically. I might have recited the First Psalm before Heathcliff replied.

"What makes you ask?" His voice was husky, whereas mine quavered.

"People do, you know."

"What for?"

"I'm not sure."

"How do you know people do?"

"I saw them."

"Who?"

"Hindley and Nelly."

"Where?"

"At Penistone Crags. Yesterday. Before you came. They were naked on the gold dust in front of the fairy cave."

He said nothing for the length of a longer psalm. Although I kept squeezing his hand, I could detect no answering pressure. Neither did he try to withdraw. Although we lay far from the edge of the loft, I felt as I had yesterday out on the jut—light-headed, giddy, weightless.

"What do you *think* made them do that?" he finally asked.

"To have a child, I think. That's how people make babies, I'm pretty sure."

Another silence. I heard mice scampering in the hay. Because the wind had died, the scent of the heath and the garden was gone, leaving the air of the barn heavy with its own reek. Still I clutched Heathcliff's unresponsive hand. My vitals were warm. My skin, even under the wet clothing, felt flushed.

"I don't believe it," he declared.

"That they did? Or that that's how babies get made?"

[42]

"Babies are made in the mother's belly. I've seen calves and pups born."

"They come out of their mother's belly, I know. But how do they get started?"

"God starts them," he replied quickly, then added, "I suppose." I could tell he was considering whether I might be right. "You remember, I told you Nelly told me so when I asked her one time about the bull mounting cows and the hounds getting hasped with the bitches. She said God made people in a different way. *He* had to give them babies, not nature. And He only gave babies to married women."

Now I didn't answer. I let him weigh the two explanations. If he decided I was right, he'd be angry, I knew. Not at me. At himself for being wrong. Not even that exactly. For believing what he was told.

"Why would Nelly want to have a baby? She's not married." His manner of asking about what he had professed not to believe made clear to me that he was beginning to believe it.

"I don't know. But why else would she put Hindley's tinkler in her mouth? I think it must be like taking food."

Suddenly Heathcliff withdrew his hand. Turning from me, he lay on his back, his palms forming a pillow for his head. From the way in which his mouth was set, lips slightly parted and pulled back from the corners so that in the semidarkness I could see the gleam of his teeth, I knew there would be no more argument, not even questions. He would make what he had to out of my revelation.

For a long while I remained on my side, watching him. All that interrupted the silence was the occasional scurrying of a mouse or the lowing of a cow out in the barton. Within, I kept churning with excitement.

"Heathcliff," I finally whispered, "I know how we can find out. For a certainty." I waited. He never stirred. Rolling toward him and putting my lips against his ear, I murmuringly asked, "Will you dare, Heathcliff, will you dare?"

While, kneeling over him, I tugged off his wet boots and stockings, he said nothing. But I read his assent in his making his limbs responsive to my undressing them, in the slight lifting of the hips I could feel. Still I had difficulty tugging

[43]

down his sopping pantaloons and drawers. The wetness made them stick to his skin. As his drawers came free, his tinkler leapt straight up. How different he was between the legs from Hindley, who had that darkness!

Heathcliff never thrashed or wrestled with me, as Hindley had with Nelly yesterday on the sand. If I hadn't felt an ever so slight throbbing with my lips, I might have thought that he was sleeping with his eyes wide and glowing in the shadow beyond the shaft of sunlight. Or that he was dead. As I tried to get from him whatever might start the baby, my vitals were warm water.

Nothing happened. I had expected to feel something come leaping from him, like a porriwiggle out of a fist, into me. But nothing happened. I was certain. That puzzled me. How could the baby get started?

At last I gave up. Indeed, my knees ached from kneeling, my neck and spine from bending. Gradually my body came back into flesh. Only when it proved impossible for me to tug his loppy drawers and pantaloons over his limbs did Heathcliff remove his hands from beneath his head. As he arose, to wriggle the garments up, with his tinkler curved and some smaller, I placed my hand in a new spot in the hay in order to push myself to my feet. My fingers and palm pressed against something large and hard. Thinking it might be the skull of a rat or of a barn cat who had died and moldered up here in the loft, I drew back my hand in a little scare. With my boot I kicked the object clear of the hay and into the sunlight at Heathcliff's feet. It was a clog.

Nearby was another. And a pair of brown worsted stockings.

SEPTEMBER 7, 1774

I lay inside the fairy cave. Waiting for Heathcliff. He didn't come. I could hear the rain outside, beating against the stone of the crags, could hear the whip of wind and feel its tail end swish. Suddenly the mouth of the cave, which had been only slightly less dark than the black depths of the interior, was lit by a crackle of fire. A split second later I was almost deaned by a thunderclap. In the silence that followed, the husky voice of Heathcliff echoed, "Cathy, Cathy."

As I heard the screak of the panels sliding apart, I woke to the realization that I had been dreaming in my oak cabinet bed. A flash of lightning through the lattice window revealed Heathcliff's face between the parted panels. Then a blast of thunder rattled the whole house. A second after the world went dark, I saw the flickering of a candle in the chamber.

"What is it, Heathcliff?" I whispered. He hadn't awakened me because he was frightened by the storm, that I knew. Now I could hear the fir cones clattering against the pane.

"Come with me," he murmured, reaching in and taking me by the hand.

Overhead I heard the clack of a pair of uneven rockers and a low-pitched moaning. Joseph rocking and praying, or cursing, up in his garret bedroom. By the light of the inch of candle Heathcliff had lit I could make out the washstand on which the candlestick stood, and more dimly the tall clothes press, the iron-hooped trunk with its rounded lid against the opposite wall, and Heathcliff's trestle bed. All at once, as a heightened scud of wind extinguished the flame, the room went black.

"Is something wrong, Heathcliff?" I asked, throwing off the bedclothes.

"Never mind," he answered, leading me by the hand. "Just be quiet and come." He made his way across the room as if he had cat vision.

As he opened the door of our bedchamber, carefully, so that its screak was ever so slight, out in the hallway I could see light coming up the stairwell from the lamps in the downstairs sitting room. The noxious fume of tobacco told me that Joseph, his short-stemmed pipe, which seemed as much a part of his mouth as his lips and tongue, clamped between the teeth of his lantern jaw, had recently shambled through the hallway to the ladder that leads to the back attic. That meant it could not be much past nine o'clock. Approaching the stairwell on tiptoe, my hand still inside Heathcliff's, I heard voices becoming louder. First I recognized Hindley's, then my father's.

Heathcliff dropped to the floor beside the banister and stretched out on his belly. Resting his chin in the heels of his upturned palms, which were propped on his elbows, he positioned his forehead between two oak spindles of the railing. I did likewise alongside him. Through my cambric nightdress, the flagstones that made up the floor of the stairwell felt cold. What with the fluttering of the lamp flames and an occasional explosion of light from the sky outside, the eight-day clock that stood on the turn of the landing seemed to be doing a wild Scottish reel. Thunder was rumbling off across the moors.

"Listen," Heathcliff whispered.

"And why, sir, may I ask, am I to be sent off so immediately?"

"Because you must secure for yourself an education," answered my father.

"And why, sir, when I would be a farmer like yourself, must I have an education?"

"I would not have a benighted son. We have enough and more of our ignorant northern farmers."

"The house holds books in plenty, if I may say so."

"Their pages are all unbroken by your fingers."

"I'll submit myself to Shielders. He'll put me through a course of reading that will sufficiently enlighten me."

"Ill-informed himself, despite his black coat and shovel hat, Shielders is scarcely fit to instruct the children in their catechism. He it is has advised me to enter you into a college. The man displays more modesty and sense than I had credited him with."

"If the curate is unequipped, then you shall be my mentor. I'll attend to your instruction, I pledge my word on it."

"Nay, I am neither dominie nor Levite. Let go my limitations, I lack inclination to instruct to the very degree that you lack discipline to submit yourself. If you are ever to be aught, you must hie to the university."

"Why now, sir, all so abruptly?"

[46]

"Your eighteenth year approaches. You must begin to act the man."

In the interval of silence I could hear the tick of the pendulum of the clock, the faint crackle of coals from the sitting room fire. I shivered, for the night air was chill, although it was only September. Thrusting my side full-length against Heathcliff's, I could feel the warmth of his body through our garments.

"Sir, if you'll forgive me, I must declare that I believe you have quite another reason from the one you give for wanting me gone from this house." Hindley's voice had turned surly.

"And what might that be, my man?"

"You have never cared for me. With my mother in the kirkyard, you wish to surround yourself only with your favorites. You have told me you think me naught, unlikely to thrive."

"The desire to have you become something more than naught and to enable you to thrive has brought me to this step. As for my predilections, there you must not concern yourself. I will have my way."

"Ah. I see, sir. So be it. Though I shall never understand how a Christian father can prefer and favor a gypsy brat over his own flesh and blood. And though it is not the place of a son to admonish his father, since we are entered on the matter, I can bite my tongue no longer. I say respectfully to you and out of brotherly heed to her welfare that by permitting my sister to run wild with that young fiend you will be guilty of her ruin. Why, the rector of the parish . . ."

"No more!" My father's voice crackled as had the lightning. "Impudent puppy! My business is my business. I shall brook no more of meddling from the surplice than from a whelp who should I choose will beg his bread. Another such impertinence and so I'll choose. You hear?"

The clock chimed the half hour, punctuating the silence that followed this outburst. As it did so, a flash of lightning lit the stairwell for an instant, bright as noon. I couldn't help wincing. Even Heathcliff, whose face flashed, then faded as I

[47]

glanced toward him, started a bit, I felt. From far across the moors thunder boomed.

"I beg your pardon, sir. I ought not have spoken so," Hindley whined. Knowing him as I did, I detected more of sarcasm than of apology in his tone. I couldn't imagine truckling with such bad grace. "Yet I plead with you not to send me from home at this juncture."

"I might turn the question around," declared my father, at a lowered pitch, "and ask, pray tell, why your great reluctance to go. At this juncture."

"The prospect of being a scholar holds no appeal for me."

"Nay, that's not sufficient. As I have explained, there's no intention of making an ecclesiast or a lawyer of you. Every gentleman owes it to himself, to whatever children he might sire, and to his nation to enlarge and discipline his mind. Such would I have you do."

"Risking your displeasure, I must repeat, the very idea is repugnant to me."

"Should you persist in such stubborn and unreasonable opposition, you will provoke more than my displeasure. You'll kindle my ire. Shall I tell you out and out what I believe? I think that entering the university is not so absolutely unattractive to you as you make it sound. Rather, to offer a fine distinction, I am convinced that your abhorrence is rather of leaving this place."

"Whatever do you mean, sir?"

"To put a still finer point on the matter, you have a strong desire, indeed a lust to remain."

"I fear I fail to understand."

"Hindley, you must not play the innocent with me."

"Play innocent? Innocent of what, pray?"

"For Heaven's sake, don't echo me. Rather, speak out truthfully, like a man. How could you believe you might allow such an attachment to develop under my very nose without having me discover it?"

"Attachment? To whom?"

"Ah, you young hypocrite. I'm too miserably ashamed to utter the name. You know full well to whom. Denial is not

[48]

only futile. It will cost you dearly. Let me remind you once more that I am the sole source of your maintenance, even at college."

Another silence. So still had the house become, except for the tick tock of the clock, that I could hear myself breathing. Or was it Heathcliff's breath I heard?

"So that hideous young monster has played both spy and informer against me. All to gain his hellish vengeance. And you vouchsafed him. Against your son. Indeed, you encouraged him by attending. I swear by the teeth of Lucifer I'll have his blood for that."

"You'll have nothing of the kind. Since we're opening our minds fully and honestly, let me give you my word as a gentleman that not a syllable concerning you that I have heard has dropped from Heathcliff's lips."

"Then it must have been that footloose, sharp-eyed, rattle-tongued chit of a girl my sister. His billie. I'll serve her a turn or two."

"Nay, again you miss the mark. Conjecture no further. Dost think my nose too old to smell what is laid directly beneath it? My eyes too dim to see? My ears too tired to hear? Hindley, Hindley, you have ruined an innocent young creature."

"Since it is out, I'll have you know I intend to make her an honest woman."

"What! You intend to make her an honest woman!" My father fairly hissed the words. As if there were some horror on his tongue. Then his voice became peremptory. "Once and for all, my man, disabuse yourself of such a fantastic notion. It is, I assure you, altogether out of your power to redeem the girl. And let me instruct you further. Already you have done not only her but yourself as well an irreparable harm. Mark you, a greater wrong than you can possibly comprehend. Here is my solemn command—that as of this instant there be no correspondence of any sort, save as master and servant, between you two."

Hindley's voice dropped so low I could make out his words only with difficulty.

"My father, I beseech you to reconsider. That I have sinned with her I freely confess. I am contrite. The only satisfaction I can offer to her and before God is that now I make her my wife."

"Hush!" my father shouted. "You speak not only nonsense but blasphemy."

"Why should my desire to make recompense by marriage be blasphemy? Believe me, young as I am and isolated as we be, I have heard enough of the world to know that many a man and lass who have married and that very happily have beforehand . . ."

"The girl is a house servant," my father broke in hoarsely. "That alone is enough prohibition."

"That matters not a whit to me, I find her pleasing."

"You know nothing of her."

"I know that before I became the instrument of her ruin she was indeed honest. And that by marrying . . ."

"She is the daughter of a clown of a crofter, unable to support his own family. If I didn't provide out of charity, moved by my fondness for the girl, who until you corrupted her had been a faithful servant, his wife would starve. As for the girl herself, she has no name, no money, no prospects. She would be your ruin."

"What care I for name or money? I have my own prospects. It is enough that I love the girl and wish to . . ."

Hindley's words broke off into a choking sound. Another fork of lightning, brighter than the lights of the seven golden candlesticks of Revelation, illuminated the stairwell. And another and another. I was staring into Heathcliff's flashing eyes. So fierce was the light that his dark face seemed pallid. Then as if it had returned to put an accursed seal on the terrible conflict between my father and my brother, a clap of thunder greater than the blast of the seven ram's horn trumpets with which Joshua tumbled the walls of Jericho shook the house till it trembled. The accompanying whirl of wind sweeping through whatever cracks or openings the place possessed extinguished the lamps in the sitting room. Perfectly still, perfectly dark stood the house.

[50]

"If you were not your mother's son by me, I swear I should murder you," my father's voice declared with a passion so subdued that it gripped me with horror.

A gasping and coughing. A banging and bumping as if furniture and the very walls downstairs were moving and colliding in the dark. A crashing and ringing of metal against stone. A tinkling of broken glass. As I leaped up in terror and ran blindly, thrusting myself into the banister and against walls until I felt out the still open door to my bedchamber, the clock struck ten. Throwing myself into the cabinet bed and smashing the panels closed behind me, I dived beneath the bedclothes and buried my face in the down mattress.

After hearing the door from the hallway screak as Heathcliff closed it behind him and then hearing Heathcliff settle into his trestle bed, I pulled the fat feathered pillow over my head.

SEPTEMBER 23, 1777

"Would you care to walk across the moor with me, Miss Catherine? I'll visit with my mother today."

In the three years since Hindley had gone off to college, Nelly had scarcely addressed me. For a full six months into this period she had not even rested her eyes upon me nor flung me a syllable. With Heathcliff, however, she had never ceased being altogether amiable. Indeed, I found her too fond of him, too familiar with him. That he tolerated her presuming intimacies, while she ignored me, was infuriating. Whenever I declared my resentment, he merely shrugged his shoulders. And, if he didn't positively encourage it, he permitted Nelly to continue her fraternization. It was as if there were some unspoken, secretly acknowledged bond between them. Since the time long ago she had nursed him through his near-fatal fever, shortly after his arrival at the Heights, it had been that way—fondness on her part, acceptance on his. I was wild with jealousy.

[51]

For my part, I had never cared for Nelly with any degree of particularity. After my mother had died, she had commenced treating me as though I were her nursling. And when I let her know I would not be ruled by her merely because she was older than I, we had open words. Indeed, on a number of occasions when she tried to enforce her authority, I responded with my hands and fingernails. After such hints, she resorted to nothing more than her tongue to hector me. We lived a cat and dog life in the house together.

I could tell that Nelly too was envious of *my* relationship with Heathcliff. Along with Joseph, whom she loathed, only making common cause with him to strengthen the side against me, whenever she might find a means to deny me Heathcliff's company, she did so. Joseph's motive was his malicious hatred of Heathcliff. We were a pretty household.

Dislike me as she did, manifest her jealousy over Heathcliff as she might, Nelly had never turned tongue, eye, and ear from me until such time as Hindley before he departed for college told her, as I'm certain he must have, that Heathcliff and I or I alone had revealed them to my father.

Even should Hindley doubt my father's assurance as a gentleman that Heathcliff was not the informer, Nelly knew Heathcliff well enough, though she would be too pawky to avow it to Hindley, to believe Heathcliff capable of taking such a low form of vengeance on Hindley and of serving her such a spiteful turn. Why she and Hindley failed to suspect Joseph, who I felt certain was in fact the agent, I could not understand. If Hindley and Nelly had brought their correspondence, as my father termed it, from the foot of Penistone Crags, where they could be certain to be remote enough to escape Joseph's corvine eye, to so close to home as the loft in the cow barn, Joseph's own demesne, what could they expect but discovery? And after that, mindful of Joseph's jaundiced view of Nelly, his sycophantic behavior toward his employer, his phariseeism, how could they imagine he would not pour his poison into my father's ear? Heathcliff and I had enough sense to make certain we kept out of Joseph's ken.

What moved Nelly, after three years of undeclared warfare,

of a sudden to offer me an olive branch was not clear. Perhaps with Hindley gone she had found herself alone for so long that finally she had become desperate for company. Except to grumble and rebuke, Joseph had no truck with her. My father, who preferred to sit with her to sitting with me—indeed, after Heathcliff, Nelly was his favorite—held himself more and more solitary, often taking his meals alone. His books provided all his companions. The smiles and approbations he regularly tendered Nelly, affectionately as they were meant, furnished her no opportunity for prattle. Perhaps, having had time to mull the Hindley affair over and finding she in no way suffered in my father's eyes from whatever revelation concerning her role had been made, she forgave me, if indeed she had deemed me the culprit. Or perhaps in time she too finally arrived at the conclusion that Joseph had betrayed Hindley and her. Perhaps, gossip that she was, she was driven, despite whatever of suspicion, resentment, and jealousy she felt, to reopen for herself the possibility of intercourse with the only other female soul in her daily vicinage.

For my part, innocent as I knew myself to be, I was not loath to agree to an armistice, less because I cared for either Nelly's society or goodwill than to relieve our circumscribed community of the tension, sometimes almost unendurable, our silent hostility had effected for so long. Besides, that Nelly had been the one to strike her colors provided me with a certain feeling of triumph. I could afford to be responsive. I did not fail to notice, however, that in prefixing the formal "Miss" to my given name, which she knew so familiarly, she reserved for herself the right to make me experience an arrogant condescension on her part and at the same time provided herself an avenue of retreat, whence she might resume the moral battle, should I reject her overture.

Ordinarily I would have no part of joining Nelly on a moor walk. She was too sedate, too tame, too devoid of imagination to engage in the sort of games Heathcliff and I still play together. Nor had I the least desire to make the acquaintance of Nelly's mother. Heathcliff supplied me with all the communion I craved or needed. But apart from my willingness to return to our former state of surface civility, I was moved to accept Nelly's offer to accompany her by the absence of Heathcliff.

Heathcliff my father had ordered to accompany Joseph to Gimmerton with a load of ripe oats. So wet had the growing and harvest seasons been this year that second planting had been delayed and the oats had greened later than usual. And now with a spell of dry weather for cutting, all the other hands were required in the fields. Abandoned to my own devices, I had been forcing myself to choose between a ramble on the moors with no prospect of being joined by Heathcliff, in which case I would feel only half the pleasure, only half alive, only half myself, and being mewed up alone in the house. Nelly's invitation relieved me of the necessity of choosing between undesirables.

Off we set, Nelly in a gray drab cloak and a gray bonnet, carrying a willow basket, I in a holland pinafore and without bonnet. Nelly had stopped caring for my hair three years ago, when she had declared unspoken war. Instead of doing my hair as she had, I simply let it fall so the ringlets tumbled onto my shoulders and fell over my eyes. Drabble-tailed, Shielders had once sneeringly called it.

The day was overcast, the all but invisible sun now smutching an amethyst circle almost directly overhead. As if a dull halo hung above the ripened earth. As we passed along the field between the farmyard and the lower portion of the wold, where sheep were cropping the grass, the tall corn the hands had not yet cut their way to stood up so decidedly golden that it seemed light was leaping out of it rather than filtering down from the sun. Higher up the moorside the thistle was knobbed with brown and the heather and bracken had just begun to sere, going toward winter's black, having been blasted and blighted by a number of fierce September storms.

Nelly's mother's home lay situated in a dale a few miles down the valley, away from Penistone Crags. On our seldom excursions in this direction, Heathcliff and I had seen it from the moor tops: within a maze of stone walls, a small rectangle of dark stone with a low-pitched roof, a squat chimney at each

[54]

extremity, narrow slits of windows, a cluster of outbuildings, all stone, within the farmyard. A single ancient lumber tree rose to maybe twice the height of the house, its sparse foliage providing little shade and little break against wind, snow, and rain.

As we plodded along at the pace of packhorses, I half a step in front of Nelly, for she's inclined to be stout and is a bit pursy, she thawed considerably, dropping the "Miss" and twaddling about domestic matters. Though she spoke of the sloth of the new dairymaid, toward whom her chidings were directed daily, the boorishness of the hands, the intolerable self-righteousness of Joseph, the "Miss Nancy-ness" of the curate, the generous though mysterious ways of my father, the growth of Heathcliff, she made no mention of the absent Hindley.

Stopping to rest for a moment at the top of a coombe within sight of our destination, she recounted to me how her family came to occupy one of my father's farms. It seems that her grandfather, her mother's father, had owned hereditary tenant rights to the place. Upon his death and her mother's marriage, both of which happened almost coincidentally, her father, who came from even poorer stock than did her mother, somehow had secured a sum of money sufficient to buy the rights from her mother's only brother, who taking this portion had shipped before the mast out of Liverpool, to be heard of nevermore. Her father's father, a very ancient man, had lived on in the farmhouse with his daughter-in-law and son until she, Nelly, had been seven or eight. She could remember seeing him, on visits home, sitting in the chimney corner, smoking a long-stemmed clay pipe, his face wizened like a dry prune, with huge hairy ears, his body shrunk, as if he were clemmed, to child's size, from which his arms and legs protruded like the appendages of a spider. He scarcely spoke. While sleeping upright, he could smoke without losing his pipe from his mouth or the fire from his pipe bowl. Her mother was considerably younger than her father, she informed me. Except for her, her parents had not been blessed with children.

Then we descended the swale to the farmyard. The gate,

for which two upright slabs of stone served as posts, dangled on a single hinge. Up close the farm looked indeed neglected, almost derelict. We passed through the yard, gray clayish soil wet enough to muddy our boots, full of stones and boulders, with tufts of knot-grass here and there, and nettle and night-shade growing along the wall of the house. So dilapidated were the outbuildings you could scarcely distinguish them from the stone fences, themselves in a deplorable state of re-pair, in which they were set. In what I took to be the barn, there was a hole from which sufficient stone had fallen on each side for me, as I passed directly in front, to be able to see clear through the building to the rise of the moor and the low sky beyond it, as if I were looking at a framed painting of the landscape.

A few scrawny geese and chickens pecked about, the geese squawking at our approach, the chickens clucking to them-selves. The din of the fowl brought a fat brindled dog, with a dirty orange ruff and its tail docked, waddling from behind the barn. He more nearly resembled a sow than a wolf. Cast-ing a tired red eye at us, he stood a moment, snapped a couple of mouthfuls of something that looked like old porridge from a battered pail, then went wobbling inside the barn, presum-ably to sleep.

Mending a shaft on a sagging wain beside a stand of hives, with rabbit warrens behind it, both deserted, was a clownish-looking old fellow with very white hair. He had on clogs, worn leather breeches, and a faded blue blouse or smock. A long-stemmed pipe was clamped between his teeth. On his narrow forehead he carried a large court-plaster, apparently covering some sort of sore or wound. From the offhand greet-ing Nelly tossed him and his incomprehensible reply—he hardly raised his eyes toward us—I took him to be a hand. Nelly showed no inclination to introduce us.

On the low-pitched roof of the house, additional thick slabs, presumably to cover leaks in lieu of repairing, lay everywhere. Unfastened though they were, they were too weighty to be blown off by the wind. The roof buckled so that its collapse into the middle of the house seemed imminent. Like that of the fences and the outbuildings, the stone of the house was irregular and set in highly uneven rows. What little lumber had been used around doors and windows and in the eaves was unpainted, weathered gray, not much less dark than the almost black stone of which the entire farm was constructed. I allowed Nelly to precede me past a row of stunted fruit trees, planted close to the back wall, under the low lintel of the kitchen door.

Though small and dark, the kitchen was tidy and spotless as a cat in pattens. A large black pot simmered on the cooking stove, built into the lefthand portion of the fireplace. The stove shone like polished ebony. Except for a large porridge thible, obviously being used for stirring, which was lying on the fender, all of the knives and spoons and spatulas and ladles hung on bent nails driven into the top of the frame of the low narrow window. Leaning against a larder, on which a piece of beef hung drying on a hook, stood a thick besom. A kettle, its brass polished to brightness, dangled on the hob in the fireplace over a bed of smoldering peat. In the center of the floor stood a deal table, with a lamp on it; on either side was a spindle-back chair. I remembered hearing my father once say about our tenant cottagers: observe the keep of the farm outside; step into the kitchen and judge its care; thus know whether the man or his woman rules the roost.

Nelly's mother sat beneath the window on a pine bench, the white-washed interior of the kitchen wall serving as a backrest, her workbasket in her lap, hemming a coarse sheet. Hearing the latch, she had looked up from her work, then seeing Nelly had resumed it. While she sewed, she was singing to herself in a soft clear voice. She wore ox-leather pattens, lisle stockings, and a plain homespun apron over a gown of mauve hopsack. At her feet lay a large Manx cat, who opened a sleepy eye as we entered, then, concluding we were no threat to his peace, closed it and resumed his nap. To the side of the bench, on two large half moons, stood a shinily varnished cradle. Although I assumed it to be Nelly's, it looked as if it had never been used.

Except that she was a couple of stones heavier than Nelly,

her weight indicating the corpulence Nelly already was tending toward, Mrs. Dean looked young enough to be her daughter's sister. And I was indeed struck by their resemblance: the same pretty little mouth, the same pudgy nose, the same large eyes. Their colorings, however, were somedeal different: whereas Nelly's hair was light brown, the identical shade of Hindley's and mine, and her skin was middling fair, Nelly's mother's hair, without a strand of gray, was so blond as to seem white, her skin very fair, her eyes so decided a blue they seemed to have been plucked from a clear June sky. Nelly's eyes were hazel. Despite her plumpness, there was a doll-like quality about Mrs. Dean. At forty, or thereabouts, she was just starting to lose her prettiness.

After finishing the stave of the song she was crooning,

> Oh, never melt awa', thou wreath o' snow
> That's sae kind in graving me;
> Nut hide me frae the scorn and guffaw
> O' villains like Robin-a-Ree!

which I recognized as the old Scotch ballad "Puir Mary Lee," Mrs. Dean laid her work aside and was about to rise and make us tea. But Nelly, after introducing me as "Mr. Earnshaw's youngest bairn so grown," prevented her by entreating her to continue her sewing and by setting about making the tea herself. Stirring the fire and throwing on some twigs and peat, she soon had the kettle at boil. From a canister, one of a neat row lined on the mantel over the fireplace, she took tea and brewed it in a teapot that stood on the table with a dainty little cream ewer and sugar bowl, and a pewter slop basin. Lettered on the side of the porcelain teapot was:

> Though your sins be as scarlet,
> They shall be as white as snow;
> Though they be red like crimson,
> They shall be as wool.

From the manner in which Nelly set to work in her mother's kitchen and from the ensuing prattle they engaged in

[58]

while we had tea with plain muffins, clapbread, and marmalade, Nelly and I drawing chairs from the table to either side of Mrs. Dean, it was evident that the two women got on easily. Indeed, they behaved together more like sisters than like mother and daughter. Mrs. Dean, I noticed, called Nelly by her baptismal name, Ellen.

Partway through our bever, I heard the sound of clogs outside on the rough stones that were laid as a walk through the mucky yard to the kitchen door. I turned to see the latch lift, the door swing into the room, and the old man who had been mending the shaft of the wagon come sluthering in. Without further acknowledging the presence of Nelly or me, he exchanged a few words with Nelly's mother in a tongue so laden with the provincial north that it seemed to be thick as an ox's. Except for some uncertain reference to the "sprat," Nelly I supposed, and "mawn-ey" and "rint-day," I could make nothing out of his gibber. I wondered whether Nelly perfectly understood the clod. Although her English was not so cultivated as Nelly's, Nelly's mother's manner of speaking presented no difficulty to me whatever.

Recollecting of a sudden that on our walk across the moor Nelly had told me about the disparity in age between her mother and her father, and putting together with that recollection the familiarity with which the old fellow addressed Mrs. Dean, I concluded for a certainty that the man I was trying to comprehend while I stared at him was Nelly's father. Not a trace of resemblance to his daughter could I find. With hair the color of frost, eyebrows so light they scarcely seemed to exist, chalk-colored skin—how could it be he earned his bread sweating beneath the sun, I wondered—he, it struck me, must be something I had read about but never seen: an albino. Whereas the irids of his eyes were colorless as milk, the eyeballs themselves were tinged red, like a rabbit's. Lean as a pitchfork, he was scarcely so tall as Heathcliff, his back bent crooked, almost humped beneath his narrow shoulders. For her part, though plump enough, Nelly tended to be tall, standing almost to the height of my father.

Nor were the striking dissimilarities merely physical. If in

Nelly's face a lively intelligence glowed—indeed, despite her humble origin and her limited opportunities, there was a look of cultivation—the old man's flat sloping forehead, squeezed between his scant eyebrows and his low hairline, his narrow foxlike face, the limp lower lip that with his slack jaw allowed the gaps between his little yellow teeth to show, and his small-boned cheeks projected a mind of narrow comprehension and mean understanding, a temperament of stolidity and torpor. Neither the piglike dog in the farmyard nor the somnolent cat by the hearth could, to my way of thinking, be less alert and lively than Mr. Dean. Here was a man, I decided, who couldn't tell cheese from chalk. How Nelly's mother, bonny as she certainly had been, had allowed such a creature to woo her, I could not help wondering. Well-spoken and sensible as she seemed, that she ever could have given herself in marriage to such a witless clown was beyond all my imagining.

After Nelly's mother, while waxing her needle as she prepared to rethread it, assured him that all was well, he slowly turned and went shambling out the door. Whereupon the three of us resumed our tea and chatter.

As we were about to make our departure, Nelly opened her willow basket, removed her purse, and extracted some bank-notes. How many I could not tell, though there looked to be a goodly sum. These she proffered to her mother, who deposited them in her workbasket without asking for an explanation or even expressing gratitude. The whole business was conducted so matter-of-factly, without a word's being uttered by either party, that I took it in my head that this transaction, rather than a sincere desire for her mother's company or filial affection, was the ultimate motive for the visit. Rising to kiss Nelly and to shake my hand, Mrs. Dean proved to be even taller than Nelly. Were she and her husband to stand side by side, surely she would have towered above him. Like her greeting and her hospitality, her farewell was cordial but restrained. Nelly, I thought, responded with the identical balance.

After I had paid her some compliments on both her mother's person and her kitchen, which she received politely enough without seizing the opportunity to praise her mother or to commiserate with her because of her hard or lonely circumstance or to express her affection for her despite their separation, Nelly and I walked on in silence. Although I, quite conspicuously to my mind, made no mention of the hodge I now was all but certain was her father, she herself ventured no remark about him, offered no explanation for his entrance and behavior, so that I might have doubted he really had slouched into and out of the kitchen.

The sun, which had burnt its way through the overcast, leaving clouds scattered across a slate-blue sky, now was sinking toward the moor tops, somber with rust-colored heather. Flushed pink itself, it was streaking the western portion of the heavens with rose streamers and ribands. The long ray of light that angled from it directly to our faces was so full of suspended motes that it seemed to be a pillar of coral.

A curiosity that made my heart beat faster, though I had no notion where it might lead, took hold of me. Although for some reason I could not define I was unable to bring myself to question Nelly about her father, I began to ask other questions of her. Perhaps because she wished to humor me, and thus to confirm the peace we had ratified by our joint excursion, she answered freely.

"Nelly, how long have you lived at the Heights?"

"Longer than you can remember."

"That I know. But when did you first come?"

"I was almost always there. I scarcely remember before that."

"What brought you to our house?"

"You're overflowing with questions this afternoon, aren't you. Well, my mother was your brother Hindley's nurse. Your brother and I are of an age, you know."

"What kept you there? Why didn't you return home with her when your mother left?"

"It seems that as Hindley and I were nursed together, we grew up together and got used to playing together. Then your father took a fancy to me and would have me about as Hindley's playmate, for there were no other children in the im-

[61]

mediate neighborhood. When I became a bit more grown, I ran errands and helped make hay and did whatever came to hand. From being there I was able to get the benefit of Hindley's lessons from the curate, Fairclough it was at that time. And being quick to learn my hornbook, soon I was able and allowed to read whatever volumes in your father's library I might choose. My aptness pleased your father so that he favored me all the more, Hindley having not the least inclination that way. I've taught myself beyond what you might think. And recognizing how scant my possibilities in life, I've disciplined myself sharply. By the time you appeared I was competent enough to take care of you, your mother being that delicate."

"But didn't *your* mother want you at home? Didn't . . .," I hesitated, then having gone thus far in so obvious a direction felt compelled to plunge ahead, "didn't your father?"

"They did, I'm sure. But in those days they were so very poor, after my mother's brother sold them his tenant rights and left for sea. Your father offered to pay my father generously for my services, young as I was. That sum was tidy enough to relieve my father of labor he was not robust enough to perform, being declined in years and ailing for as long as I can remember. And your father continues his largess to this day. The bestowal, made each rent day, is ordinarily carried by the dairymaid, who distributes milk allotments to the tenant farmers. But Rebecca, you remember, was married of late, though too late as it seems, for a woman must eat as she bakes and drink as she brews. Little Sarah, who has replaced her, is so young and spoonish your father would not trust her with the notes. So it left me to go. It was time I visited my mother again, regardless."

Nelly stopped for breath halfway up a hill. In order to encourage her to continue, I halted abreast of her, governing my pace by hers. While she leaned against a pile of stones that at one time had doubtless been a wall, she breathed in and out heavily, either gasping or sighing. As we started up again, she resumed her gossiping.

"Since we have come this far in matters that until now I have considered beyond your years, I think it proper you know that, seeing how I, though a woman grown, still render all the harvest of my services to my enfeebled father and my mother, your father does not allow me to go penniless. In addition to slipping something into my pocket every rent day, he never neglects to hand me a Christmas box nor forgets to present me with a birthday remembrance. And you yourself are witness that whenever he would bring you and Hindley a gift upon returning home from one of his journeys, he never would forget me. In my eyes your father is the soul of goodness and generosity."

While she was offering this testimony to the heretofore to me unknown philanthropy of my father, eulogizing him so as to do justice to a saint, I studied her in profile. The sun and the shaft of light that dropped from it onto the two of us had deepened to crimson. Illuminated as it was, Nelly's face, while partaking obviously of her mother, bore another resemblance I could recognize but not identify. That steep forehead, those high cheekbones, that chin with just the trace of a cleft, those eyes so much more deeply set than her mother's. All at once in that blood-colored light I noticed something I had never seen before: in the bottom of the irid of her left eye was a dot, so small and so slightly darker than the rest of the hazel as to be invisible, except under scrutiny in direct sunlight.

I could not look away from that fleck. My heart was pounding, not from the exertion of the walk but from the excitement of feeling myself on the brink of a precipice that offered a view of a hitherto unbeheld prospect. Sensing my stare, Nelly turned toward me, so that we gazed at each other full-face.

"What is it, Catherine?" she asked.

Whether Nelly herself knew whose child she was, I was unable to tell. If she indeed did know, whether she could read in my visage that at that precise instant I also knew I was beholding my half-sister, I could not decide. I smiled. At least I made myself try to smile, while holding back a torrent of hot tears. My smile, I fear, must have looked more like the twisted expression on the face of a soul that is being entered by a sharp, red-hot iron.

"I'm glad we're friends again," I managed to whisper, though on the broad moor slope there was not even a sheep close enough to hear a shout.

It wasn't until we crossed the field, by this time mowed to stubble, which now stood purple in the light the world had turned since the sun had dropped behind the top of the swell, that I uttered to myself the last dark truth to emerge on this momentous afternoon and evening: if Nelly is my father's daughter, she is also Hindley's sister.

[2]
Testament

SEPTEMBER 24, 1777

We lay naked on the sand. The sky began incredibly far away. And stretched endlessly. So clear was the atmosphere that Penistone Gorge was a funnel of light. At the top of the funnel the stone of the crags shone golden. The underside, beneath the jut, was a dark hollow. A great shag of moss, deep green and purple and black, at one place clung to the cliff-side.

Last night, as lying in bed I heard the wind, which had sprung up as breeze from the southwest in early evening, driving the clouds northward and eastward, I knew the weather would be fair when I awoke. I had closed the panels of the oak cabinet. Heathcliff lay in the room outside, in his trestle bed.

For the first time since our life together had begun, there was something I was reluctant to tell him. From late afternoon, when he had returned with Joseph and the wagon from Gimmerton, until I had fallen asleep, I had been on the point of opening my mind about Nelly to him a dozen times. Each time a stone stood on my tongue, a stone I could neither spit nor swallow. The stone was a huge heavy fear, fear that should I tell him, the stone itself would come between us and keep us apart. That not because he'd think the less of me for my father's having gotten a bastard on a country woman. Heathcliff, I knew, subscribed to Joseph's "visiting the iniquity of the fathers upon the children" morality not a whit more than did I.

Nor was it that the idea of Nelly's being my father's daughter and thus sister to Hindley and me had come so suddenly and was so immense that, being unable to take it in and make it part of myself, I had allowed it to overwhelm me and transform me into another being, someone Heathcliff did not know. Unsuspected and shocking as the discovery was, I neither thought the less of my father nor found myself threatened. Indeed, the revelation threw a backward light on the dark scene between Hindley and my father that Heathcliff and I had overheard as we lay side against side at the top of the stairwell during that terrible lightning storm; it made as clear as the present light on Penistone Crags why my father had had to separate Hindley and Nelly by packing Hindley off to college. It also accounted for Nelly's ancient and continuing presence at the Heights, for my mother's coldness toward and sullen treatment of her, for my father's favoring her. Beyond finding my tongue checked by a fear whose shape I could no more define than a blind man could a mountain's, but which was as substantial to me as a mountain, I could not account to myself for my inability to tell Heathcliff.

Whether Nelly herself knew who had fathered her I still could not decide. The freedom with which she had informed me of how she had come to and had stayed at the Heights and of my father's apparently disinterested philanthropy would argue that she did not. And her homilies on poor Rebecca, the milkmaid who a month since had been married to one of the hands and already had presented him with a bairn, would indicate that she was ignorant of her own unfortunate begetting.

But Nelly I well knew was full of disguise and guile, was able to play contrary parts with perfect ease. Should the occasion ask for them, moral sentiments would flow from her mouth as freely as water over the splash after a heavy rain. Yet she was far too canny and realistic to believe in or live by such platitudes. To my way of thinking, she was an utter skeptic. And if it were impossible to discover the principles or policies by which Nelly governed her life, so I knew there was no greater likelihood of penetrating her mask and learning whether she knew whose child she was. Between her and me there seemed no possibility of confidences being exchanged. In short, Nelly would be sister and no sister at once. If for some deeply troubling reason I could not reveal such a momentous discovery about the household to Heathcliff, assuredly I should not tell Nelly.

So in a perturbed and disturbed, an excited and anxious, an undefinably fearful state, I had slid the panels of the oak cabinet together behind me as I had climbed into bed, sealing myself off from the rest of the world—from the clodhopper who supposedly was Nelly's father, from Nelly's mother, from Nelly's and my father, from my brother Hindley, from Nelly herself, even from Heathcliff. I had lain listening to the rising wind as it moaned louder and louder out across the moor, had heard the fir cones knocking more insistently by the minute against the closed casement window beside my head, had watched through the pane until I had seen a radiance of thin light from the orange moon, hanging low and lopsided, dispersing the clouds. Then I had made out a scattering of stars. Confident it would be clear on the morrow, I had fallen asleep.

Now Heathcliff and I were on our sides, lying head to feet, on the shining sand under a glorious sun. Without being hot, it was warm, September weather. Our clothes in little piles served as our pillows. As he had a number of times lately, Heathcliff had just pulled himself away from me, so as to let me know that for the time we were finished. His doing so was puzzling to me, for the manner in which he removed himself was not the old way, in which having reached a point of mutual boredom simultaneously, after a long delicious period of play, we would of one accord fall apart. This new manner of disengagement was entirely one-sided. Indeed, this day we had scarcely commenced. Almost as if he had experienced a sudden sharp pain, he had jerked himself from me and pushed me off. As I had each previous time this disturbing new separation had been effected by him, I reversed my position so that we came head to head, then lay on my back beside him. Though his pizzle, as he had taught me to call it, still stood up like the guidepost at the cross path, pointing toward the sun, I refrained from any further touching.

A long time we lay so. From all the recent rain, the water from the gill that ran down the crease of the valley and coursed over the falls thumped heavily as it landed on the rocky bed in the opening of the near side of the gorge. So empty was the air that the crash seemed next to my right ear. From somewhere in the holm on through the crevice on the far side of the gorge a cushat was moaning. Though the bird had to be a distance downstream, its call seemed close to my left ear, for there was no wind, not the least breeze to carry it away from me or to impede it. Crammed with light and damped by the splashing running water, the air smelled as if it had just been created.

Perplexed as I was, indeed hurt, by Heathcliff's sudden withdrawal, I inconspicuously edged farther from him so that a corridor lay between our naked sides. Unable to penetrate his reserve, frustrated by my supposes as to what he was thinking and feeling, I took my mind back to the day on which, looking down from that treacherous jut at the top of the cliff, I had seen Nelly and Hindley naked where Heathcliff and I now lay. Recalling that it was Nelly who had taught me how to do Heathcliff, I shuddered. Perhaps, I thought, Heathcliff is growing tired of our affectionate play, is beginning to discover that I bore him, is finding that no longer do I provide him pleasure. The possibility struck me so cold in my marrow that despite the warmth of the sun I shivered.

Considering my insufficiency, I recalled how childish I had been. I remembered having told Heathcliff that Nelly and Hindley had put themselves in a way to have a child. I remembered calling Heathcliff's pizzle his tinkler, as either my mother or Nelly, I couldn't recollect which, had taught me to call the opening between my legs. From one of the hands Heathcliff had learned the proper word for the collop of flesh he had and I did not. I also remembered thinking that the shadowy patch I saw between Nelly's and Hindley's legs was dark skin. Not until a few months past, while gazing at Heathcliff's nether parts, something which always pleased and excited me, as we lay in a shaft of light in the loft of the cow barn—we had just watched gleg-eyed Joseph go off with my father to the market at K——did I realize that what I was seeing was black hair beginning to sprout. At first the sight had been hard to get used to, as if a clump of dark weeds had come poking up through the sweep of golden sand on which we were lying.

Later, touching myself in the comparable place on my body, I felt a patch of fuzz, like new moss, which showed when I scrutinized it in sunlight as brown down. I remembered noticing too that my left breast had begun to swell, like a pippin in early summer, although the right, to my consternation and embarrassment, seemed to remain as flat as Heathcliff's. I desperately hoped that Heathcliff, who had taken to sucking my nipples, so that they tingled pleasurably, would not notice the disparity. Recalling a song I had overheard one of the hands sing to the laughter of others about a cow that had only one tit and hair on her chest, I was terrified that I should grow into such a monster and that then Heathcliff would have nothing more to do with me. Again I shivered and shuddered. Had his rejection of me commenced?

"You may touch me with your hand, if you like, Cathy," Heathcliff suddenly murmured.

With an inner sigh of relief I rolled onto my side and curved my fingers around him. No sooner had I done so than his left hand wrapped itself around mine and started my palm riding up and down, in the rhythm of a fast-gaited trotting horse. My eyes were riveted on his nether self. In the clear, transparent light the black hairs looked like a copse of Scotch fir saplings on a distant hillside. As my hand, governed by his, went beyond the speed of a canter, I couldn't understand why he didn't cry out in pain. I felt ready to burst with excitement.

Suddenly I heard a curlew cry close to my ear and I saw white go jetting skyward out of Heathcliff. Then, as my innards turned liquid, milk thick as honey oozed, flowed down over my fingers, like cream running over the side of a scone.

[69]

The milk felt sticky as fresh-made treacle, and warm. As Heathcliff began moaning like the cushat, I realized that the curlew's cry had sprung from his throat.

When I lifted my eyes to his, those black circles in his bulging eyeballs looked ready to burst into dark fire and go shooting off toward the sun. My body, which had been stretched taut, sank and my nether cheeks settled onto my ankles. Although the moaning had ceased, Heathcliff's lips still formed a perfectly round "o." He seemed to be sucking on the insides of his cheeks.

Now the only sound was the crash of water. And in the air was the pungent smell of overripe fruit.

SEPTEMBER 25, 1777

The instant the curate dismissed us we bolted into the back kitchen and scurried out through the door to the garden. Although Joseph had the hands stacking corn in a far field, the one halfway up the slope rising toward Thrushcross Grange, there always was the chance he would return in midmorning and ask my father to let him appropriate Heathcliff, who could perform the work of any man, for the rest of the day's labor. As we passed the old pear tree, its boughs weighed low with their ripe load, in the yard between the kitchen and the wash-house, we hurriedly plucked some pieces of fruit and Heathcliff stuffed them into the pockets of his small-clothes. Then we headed in a direction that took us away from the field where the corn was being stacked.

A ranny wind from the north and east was driving in clouds from the horizon. As we climbed the swell, the moor was successively in sunlight and shadow. By the minute we could feel the air growing heavier with the scent of mown hay and ripe fruit. From the top of the hill we could see mist beginning to gather in Gimmerton Valley.

At the bottom of the other side of the rise, we passed through a spinney of pines and firs whose undergrowth consisted of briar and bramble and vines and creepers. As we plunged into the copse, a whole colony of blackbirds took wing with a thunderclap of beating and went flying off thick as a storm cloud. In among the trees the dappled light kept shifting. One instant it was bright here, dark there, the next dark almost everywhere, the next quite light again. Taking care not to prick or scratch ourselves, we made our way slowly. Emerging on the far side of the spinney a few steps ahead of me, Heathcliff pointed to a huge tangle of blackberries.

"I'll pick some and we can eat them with the pears," he said. "Make your apron into a basket."

Plentiful as the berries were, he soon had my apron sagging with the fruit, as his pockets were bulging with pears. When we left the edge of the woods and went on, I, clutching my apron by the fringe, had to go more slowly.

On this side of the spinney was a slade, grassy with thick splotches of purple—late thistle and willow herb, wild aster, foxglove, knobweed. Here on the bank of a beck that meandered through the meadow we sat down. With the sun, when it appeared, almost directly overhead, we made a meal of pears and berries. While the pears were slightly tart, the over-ripe berries were cloyingly sweet. I ate fewer than Heathcliff. The pungent aroma of pears spread around us, keener than the smell of the turf. When Heathcliff had had his fill of berries, I climbed down the bank and flung my apron so that the remainder of the fruit fell into the brook.

Where the blackberries had bellied in my apron a large purple stain had spread. In order to forestall a harangue from Nelly about my mucky ways, I untied the strings and, going down on my knees among the sedge, washed the apron in the clear rushing water of the beck. Scrub as I might, the purple would not come out. At last, despairing of cleansing the garment, after wringing it dry as I could, I walked back to the edge of the spinney and tied it to a low branch of a pine. It thrashed in the spirited breeze like a bicolored ensign that had been dampened by rain.

As I headed back, I heard a rustle in the woods behind me.

Turning, I saw Heathcliff, whom I had not noticed return to the spinney, carrying a log on his shoulder. The log was completely covered with brownish green moss. I waited for him. Together we walked to a hollow that had been gouged in the meadow. Heathcliff threw the log down in and led me after it by hand.

Because the grass and forb-covered ground was still damp, despite this being the third day without rain, the second of sunshine, we made a pallet of our clothes—Heathcliff's smock and small-clothes and my frock and holland petticoat and both our undergarments, even our stockings—as we removed them. The log served as our bolster. Beneath my head it felt surprisingly soft; the wood under the thick moss must have been spongy. Lying as we were in a dent beneath the level of the slade, a little basin deep enough to protect us from the wind, which we could hear rushing above us, we felt secure from any eye except one that might look down on us directly from above, as every so often between the shuffling clouds the sun did. Despite the increasing wind and clouds, the day was quite warm.

Even as we lay side by side without touching, I could sense my vitals beginning to soften. Feeling unsure, I waited for Heathcliff to proceed. Yet so fierce a want did I know that it seemed something was gnawing on my heart. We lay for a spell of time.

While I watched, the balance of color overhead shifted from blue to white to gray. Momently the sky was lowering toward the earth. Already it seemed to be touching the round edge of the world only miles beyond the rim of the dimple in which we were couched. I could still taste and smell the pungency of pears.

All at once Heathcliff slid his hand between my head and the mossy bolster and guided me by the nape of the neck. I took him nervously. We did not go head to feet as ordinarily we would. Rather, I bent over him. One of his hands then began cupping and pressing and rolling the breast that was growing and his other hand began currying the down that was just beginning to moss on me. Inside I felt warm and watery.

Again Heathcliff pushed me off and away. I resisted this

[72]

time, groping blindly. But he was stronger than I. Falling back, so that my head pillowed on the log, I lay for an instant of agony. The air was laden with pear smell. Every breath I drank in was crammed with life. I could bear the separation no longer.

"Heathcliff," I cried, "I dare you! I dare you to, I dare you. It's the devil's hole within. I dare you, Heathcliff, I dare you!"

With that I rolled onto my knees, bent my legs, and straddling him with my body straight up, I drove myself forward and down, pushing myself onto him until I felt a tearing inside and a flash of pain. At the very instant I flung myself off him, he flew up, caught me in his arms, which wrapped me like hoops of iron, heaved me over, and, dropping my back on the sod with my head again on the mossy log, he doubled my knees, tore them asunder with his hands, and plunged into me.

For a split instant I again felt a shoot of pain. Then I went tumbling over the edge of the gorge, falling down air so thick it seemed to be arresting my descent, to plunge into the black pool at the bottom. I myself transformed to water. Blind and deaf, all I was was feel. The feel was warm.

———————

The odor of ripe pears. First I smiled. Then my eyes opened a slit. To see dark gray sky domed close above me. The wind, which the earthen sides of the dimple shielded us from, whistled and roared. Heathcliff, I remembered, and I said to myself, Heathcliff. My hand, reaching for him, touched cloth. I turned my head toward where he had lain beside me, to find him gone.

Unable, though I desperately wanted to, to prevent the feel of my flesh from returning, I closed my eyes again. Gradually I sensed that my head was resting on a spongy pillow, that pieces of balled and lumped clothing lay under my back on the turf, that the stiff culm and dry tips of some bent brushed against one cheek. Between me and the bowl of the sky Heathcliff's face appeared. His black hair dangling down his forehead, his black eyes smoldering behind the locks of hair, his teeth white between his slightly parted lips.

"Are you all right, Cathy?"

[73]

"What happened?" I asked in reply.

"You fell into a fainting fit," he answered. Then added, "I think."

With that he turned from my face, leaned over me and put something cold and wet between my legs. I felt shock for an instant. Hearing a moan come out of my mouth, I cut it off. Heathcliff patted the cloth, which was no longer cold, against me. Then he withdrew it, turned it around, and replaced it. The fresh side was scarcely cool. And felt rough. After a time he removed the cloth and stood up. In his hand I saw that the gray of the cloth was streaked bright red. Heathcliff headed for the brook.

When he returned, again he mopped between my legs with the wet cold cloth. It was his muslin drawers he was using. Three or four more times he rinsed the cloth and daubed me. As the pain subsided into an ache, I was content to lie there and be done to.

"It's stopped," he said at last. "At least it's almost stopped." Still he let me lie for a time.

When at last he helped me to my feet, I was prepared for a new onslaught of pain. But it was more unsteadiness than hurt. Not a murmur escaped me though dressing myself took every ounce of my will. Heathcliff pulled his pantaloons over his naked loins. Then, knotting his bright red drawers around a large stone, he dropped them into a little pool in an eddy of the brook. However, the pool wasn't deep enough nor the water opaque enough to make all of the scarlet disappear. Down in the pool stood a circle of blood, a red irid within an eye.

I walked leaning on Heathcliff's arm, with his other arm around my middle. When we reached the tree on the edge of the spinney where my apron lashed in the wind, Heathcliff untied it from the branch and retied it around my waist. The purple stain had dried into the cloth.

Heathcliff paced himself to my slow gait. I had never known him to be so tender. Now the bottoms and low places were white with mist. As I labored up the slope of the moor on the other side of the woods, the whole world slanted pre-

[74]

cariously. And when from the foot of the hill I glanced at the Heights, situated far enough up still not to be enveloped by the creeping fog, all of the stones in the maze of walls looked about to go toppling over. The outbuildings and the house itself seemed on the point of tumbling to pieces, their stones about to avalanche down the slope, crushing and burying Heathcliff and me.

While we were still a considerable distance from the yard, Nelly, who apparently had been waiting and watching, spied us. She was bonnetless, and her long wheat-colored hair streamed behind her in the wind as she hurried toward us through the gate, as fast as her stout body would allow her legs to carry her.

"Halloo, Heathcliff," she shouted, "halloo, Catherine! Come running. Your father has been stricken."

SEPTEMBER 27, 1777

Not until today, two days after Joseph had carried him to his bed the afternoon he was afflicted, did my father speak comprehensibly again. Although I had observed that he was prone to colds and catarrhs, at which times he would often be racked by a cough and become scant of breath, my father had always been an active and otherwise healthy man. He was taller, more slender than Hindley, who being short, plump, and small-boned resembled our mother. Yet though he was lean, somewhat shallow in the chest, and gaunt-faced, my father carried broad square shoulders, like Heathcliff. A great walker, he would think nothing of traveling on foot to K____ and back of a morning and afternoon. A trip to Liverpool was but a three-day journey for him. Although after my mother's death he had turned more solitary and sedentary, sitting by the hour in the chimney corner, reading and meditating, until Hindley had gone off to college he had often mown and stacked corn side by side with Joseph and the hands. Growing as he was, Heathcliff now seemed to be replacing my father in the fields.

Toward the end of last winter my father had come down with one of those debilitating colds. At first he had paid it no heed, carrying on his everyday life. But at last the fever rendered him so weak he was forced to keep to his bed. I can remember how brightly his eyes shone, the dark spot in the left irid positively glistening, and how flushed were his cheeks. Despite my father's protests, Kenneth, the doctor, was summoned from Gimmerton by Nelly. Immediately he administered leeches and left draughts and pills, which only Nelly's iron insistence prevailed upon my father to receive. And Kenneth returned every other day to see how his patient fared and every so often to administer a clyster.

For ten days the fever raged. After it broke, my father mended slowly yet surely, and all spring and summer seemed much like himself, though leaner than ever. He did continue to suffer spasms of coughing through both plantings and down into the fall harvest, however.

When Nelly led me to his chamber, which reeked of camphor and burnt vinegar, the afternoon he bled from the mouth, I beheld naught but the ghost of my father lying in the large oak bedstead. Except for a spot on each cheek that was the crimson of the valences hanging from iron rings on iron rods around the bed, his flesh looked wasted as melted wax. While his eyes in their deep sockets glowed like clinkers in a cavernous fireplace within a dark room, his body beneath the counterpane looked skeletal. I was struck with horror. Beside the washstand with his waistcoat off and the cuffs of his shirtsleeves turned up, mixing some draughts from vials in a tumbler, stood Kenneth.

Nelly guided me to the ladderback chair with a rush seat beside the fireplace. Warm as the day was, a fire of coal and peat had been laid and now was hissing. When I could no longer endure to gaze at the blanched and shrunk face of my father, I studied the intricate pattern in the brown drugget carpet, trying to make out the principle of its flowery design. In vain. The conviction that with Heathcliff in the hollow of

[76]

the glade I had committed the sin against the Holy Ghost, the one unpardonable sin, and that thus I was responsible for my father's being smitten seized me and shook me till I trembled.

Terrierlike, it would not let go. Indeed, I knew with certitude that his hemorrhage had commenced on the tock that followed the tick on which my own bleeding had begun. Although I uttered no sound, tears of remorse and grief welled burning in my eyes, flowed over the rims, and ran scalding down my cheeks to the corners of my mouth. I tasted salt.

All at once I heard a wheezing sound issue from my father. I believed he was trying to say, "Heathcliff." In the suddenness of Nelly's revelation, the shock and horror of seeing my father struck down, the subsequent guilt and sorrow and fear I had experienced, I had forgotten about Heathcliff. As I had gone running ahead, either he had not followed me of his own volition or else Nelly had turned him aside. Again my father produced that hoarse wheezelike word. Watching his lips this time, I was quite certain he was trying to pronounce Heathcliff's name.

Before I was able to communicate my conviction that my father was asking for Heathcliff to Nelly, who evidently had not distinguished the name contained in my father's labored utterance, my father was shaken by a paroxysm of coughing. So violent was the seizure that a crimson flush overspread his face, his eyeballs rolled, his bones seemed to be dancing in the bed. I believed the end had come. So apparently did Kenneth, for I saw him signal with his head to Nelly, who was standing across the bedstead from him, that I should be removed from the room. While Kenneth held a napkin to my father's trembling lips, Nelly hurried around the footboard to where I sat and tried to lift me to my feet by the arm. I refused to budge.

"Come, Catherine," she whispered, gripping me harder and attempting to force me, "Mr. Kenneth thinks you best leave."

I clenched my teeth and shook my head. When she persisted, squeezing and tugging me with all her might, I reached out and pinched the heavy underflesh at the top of her arm as hard as I could. With a suppressed cry she let go of me and backed off a step. The glow of the little dark spot in the bottom of her left eye grew brighter as she glared at me; it recalled to me that the man who was rattling his life out in the canopied bed was also her father. As Kenneth removed the handkerchief from my father's lips, I saw it was spotted with fresh blood.

My father did not die. Gradually the coughing subsided. All that night Kenneth remained by his side. Lying awake in my cabinet bed, listening, I stared out the lattice window at the moon, full heavy it was, hanging low in the sky, like the udder of a cow wanting to be milked. Its color was flesh-pink.

In the morning Kenneth informed us that the hemorrhaging had stopped when the fever had broken just after midnight. Bleary-eyed and obviously knocked up, he left, assuring us he would return each afternoon to measure his patient's condition. Although my father slept most of the time and seemed but barely conscious even when his eyes were open, I spent hour after hour sitting in the room with him. Nelly, who was busy with household chores, appeared at specified times to administer draughts and pills, and morning and evening to hold to my father's lips a little warm brandy and water.

For the first time this morning, he allowed me to feed him a couple of spoonfuls of whey, water, and gruel, though I myself was feeling somewhat indisposed. During the night I had awakened with a seizing pain in my belly. After tossing and turning for what seemed hours, I had fallen fitfully back to sleep. Only to come awake again before dawn with the same grabbing and squeezing inside me, still more severe. On first climbing out of bed, I felt the chamber spinning around me, the floor rising and falling away. After breakfast, feeling no better, I hurried, dizzy and aching, up to my father's bedroom.

I thought he looked to be a bit improved. With a bolster placed against the headboard for support, he had got himself into a sitting position. Some of the color from those spots on his cheeks seemed to have gone back into his lips. Although the cough had not vanished, it was much diminished both in frequency and in intensity, no longer racking his whole body

[78]

into spasms. Even his eyes had lost that preternatural glow. After feeding him the thimble of breakfast, I had barely settled myself in the chair by the window with a book when I heard him distinctly say, "Heathcliff."

Laying aside my book, I hurried to his side and brushed back the dark curly locks, just beginning to gray, from over his eyes. Beneath my fingers his bushy eyebrows felt lifeless as winter grass. Then I curved my hand lightly across his forehead, as much to steady myself as to comfort him, for I still felt strangely giddy and experienced those clutching pains in my stomach. His skin was cool as a toad's.

"Are you asking for Heathcliff, father?" I asked softly.

He closed and opened his eyes, a motion I took to signify yes.

"Would you like to have Heathcliff visit you?"

This time, ever so slightly, his head inclined forward from the bolster.

I wobbled off toward the kitchen, having to steady myself on the banister as I descended the stairs, and doubling myself over as I walked in order to relieve the tightness that constricted me so in my innards. I intended to tell Nelly she must order Joseph, who without my father's express command had taken over Heathcliff all day for farm work, to release Heathcliff from wherever he was applied in order that he appear before my father. Without flinging a word back to me—she had not addressed me since I had pinched her at my father's bedside—Nelly donned shawl and bonnet and vamped off to fetch Heathcliff from the fields. I dragged myself back upstairs to my father's chamber, where I found myself more than glad to drop again onto the chair. It was as if my vitals were dough and a hand were kneading it.

When Heathcliff arrived, sweat glistening on his swarthy forehead, against which his damp black locks were plastered, spears of golden grain clinging to his smock, I watched my father's eyes dart onto his face, the most energetic motion I'd seen him engage in since he'd been stricken. The fondness with which they rested there was unmistakable. A pang of

[79]

envy, resurrected from the past, shot through my breast, causing me for the instant to forget the hand gripping my belly. Not since I had begun so faithfully to attend him, forsaking even Heathcliff in order to be in his presence, had my father looked at me with such affection. And now that Heathcliff had come he was ignoring me completely. It seems I had not mastered my jealousy after all.

Partially out of sickness over my rejection, partially because of the clutching I felt in my entrails, which seemed to come in waves, each more aggravating than the last, I determined to retreat to my bed for the remainder of the morning in hopes I should be recovered by afternoon. Without informing him of my indisposition, I asked Heathcliff whether he would stay with my father until dinner. Agreeing, he took my chair as I went swaying off. Just before passing through the doorway, I glanced back at my father. His eyes were basking on Heathcliff, who sat beside the window with sunlight pouring over him, as if he were a source of healing, a reservoir of vital force. A fit of rage grabbed and shook me.

Half blind and staggering I made my way down the hall and stumbled into my chamber. Sliding open the panels of the oak cabinet and flinging back the bedclothes, I was about to let myself fall onto the mattress when a large scarlet spot upon the sheet caught my eye. The hand inside me squeezed so tight I thought I would swoon. To steady myself I took hold of the ledge of the window sill and leaned across the bed, looking down. I stared at the stain. Somehow, I thought, I must have cut myself during the night, and hurriedly drawing up the counterpane in the dusky light in which I had arisen, I had failed to notice the scarlet spot at the time. It occurred to me that loss of blood, for the sheet was widely covered, might account for the weakness, the dizziness, and the queasiness I had been experiencing all morning. From the position of the stain on the sheet I concluded that the cut must be on my thighs or belly.

Dropping into a sitting position on the edge of the bed, my head and body within the cabinet, my legs and feet outside in the chamber, I slipped out of the list slippers I had been wearing and hiked up the skirts of my pinafore and petticoat, then tugged off my drawers. They were damp—and to my horror they proved to be covered with blood. Instinctively my fingers went feeling the crevice inside my nether lips, where three days before Heathcliff had driven his pizzle and made me bleed. They came out crimson wet. To realize that the wound had broken open again—for I had been certain the bleeding had completely stopped the night my father was felled—and that I was losing blood fast and freely turned me cold with fear.

Still clutching my red-stained drawers, I fell back upon the sheet, drew up my legs, and pulled the panels of the cabinet crashing closed. As my stomach churned with fear, a whirlwind of guilt sent the cabinet reeling madly about my head. Not only had my commission of the unpardonable sin wrought vengeance in the form of my father's hemorrhaging nearly to his death, but I myself was being bled as fitting punishment. Indeed, I had plunged myself onto the very instrument of my own destruction.

I fell either asleep or into a faint. Upon awakening, I experienced horror at what I had done, felt dread at what was to come flood over me instantly again. But the world around me had stopped spinning and the fisting and unfisting in my innards was occurring less frequently and was occasioning less pain. From the length and the angle of the shadows of the firs, which I could measure through the casement window when I pulled myself to a sitting position by gripping the ledge, I concluded that it was late afternoon. To discover whether the wound in my crevice might have healed over once more, stopping the flow of blood, I probed myself with my fingers. They emerged wetly red.

As I lay in misery unspeakable, suddenly I remembered having read in the Gospels of the woman who for twelve years had had an issue of blood. Among the books I kept piled in the corner of the wide window ledge, which served as bookcase and repository for my writing desk, was the Testament on

[81]

whose flyleaf and in whose margins I have been keeping this journal. After considerable rooting I came upon the story as recorded by St. Mark:

> And a certain woman, which had an issue of blood twelve years,
> And had suffered many things of many physicians, and had spent all that she had, and was nothing bettered, but rather grew worse,
> When she had heard of Jesus, came in the press behind, and touched his garment.
> For she said, if I may touch but his clothes, I shall be whole.
> And straightway the fountain of her blood was dried up; and she felt in her body that she was healed of that plague.

The account provided small comfort. How, I asked myself, could the woman, also apparently having committed the unpardonable sin, have bled for such a period of years without losing all of her blood and dying? It could only be that compared to the quantity of blood that had gushed from me in a few hours, her flow was a trickle, mere drops. Furthermore, it seemed clear that had she not been healed by a miracle, she would have continued to issue blood. In this day, I well knew, miracles no longer were performed.

I had to take some steps. To continue to lie there bleeding at such a rate meant certain death. I desperately needed to tell someone. Because of the deep shame I felt, I could not confide in Heathcliff. Even had my father not been stricken, and that as a result of the very sin I would have to confess, I could not bear to acknowledge to him what I had done and cause his face to becloud. Had my mother still been living, I doubted that I could have brought myself to resort to her. That turned my mind onto Nelly.

I considered how I had never had more that a rickety friendship with Nelly, how we had always been wrangling and contending. I considered the rupture in our relations within the household for the almost three years since my father had sent Hindley off to college. I considered how by vigorously using my fingers on the flesh of her arm two days previous as she had tried to eject me from my father's chamber, when it

[82]

appeared he was in his death throes, I had broken the armistice Nelly had deigned to propose and I had agreed to by accepting her offer to accompany her on that momentously revelatory visit to her mother. All of these impediments I heaped in the pan on one side of the scales. In the other I dropped the newly discovered fact that Nelly was my sister and the urgent need I had of someone. The scale of judgment inclined in favor of my attempting to confide in her. I slid open the panel doors.

Using my bloody drawers, I staunched myself until I seemed momently dry, then put on a pair of clean drawers which I took from the black press. The soiled red undergarment I flattened on the sheet of my bed, and I drew the top bedclothes up over the stained sheet and the drawers, and again closed the panels. As I made my way out into the hall, I did feel somewhat better grounded, though directly over my eyes my head was pounding. The pain in my innards, no longer a wave of sharp seizures, had become constant. Passing my father's bedroom, I saw that Heathcliff still sat in the chair by the window, now deep in shadow.

Descending the staircase, I proceeded gingerly. In the back kitchen Nelly stood at her ironing. When I came wambling in she refused so much as to glance in my direction. Stumbling over the bootjack so that I almost fell as I passed on my way to the settle, I was glad enough to lie down so soon again.

"Nelly," I commenced, deciding it was preferable to launch directly into an account of my trouble rather than first attempt to appease her anger by expressing contrition and appealing for forgiveness, "I fear I'm deathly ill."

"Hmph," she snorted, dropping the hot iron with a sizzle on the dampened article of clothing she was pressing. When the hiss had trailed off, the kitchen was so silent I could hear the mantel clock ticking.

"I think that somebody in the household ought to know what is wrong with me and that I might die. I can't burden my father, ill as he is."

"A pity for you. I dare say that young ladies who are so free

[83]

with their fingers as to turn other people's flesh black and purple ought not to expect sympathy from their innocent victims, no, not one grain of pity."

"You misunderstand me, Nelly. I'm asking for no sympathy. If I'm to die, I'll do so without a murmur. Yet I'm not so inhuman I would die in the house without advising someone of the possibility."

"Hush, miss" she hissed, sounding like the iron, which she so manipulated that it emitted an echo to her hiss. "With your father scarcely having both feet in the land of the living, for a blooming young body like you to talk of dying is little short of blasphemy."

"I tell you, Nelly, whatever you may think, I am this very moment afflicted by a disorder that drains the life from me. There now, you have it from my lips."

Hefting the iron and holding it, flat-bottom up, in midair, her arm doubled, her elbow planted on her ample hip to support the weight, Nelly looked at me doubtsomely. "I warrant there's more cry than wool in the business," she declared, seeming ready either to throw the iron at me in anger or to let it fall to the floor out of concern. "Pray tell, what is this life-threatening affliction you find yourself suffering under, Miss Catherine?"

I heaved a deep breath and swallowed before I could make myself utter the words. "I bled the bed last night. I'm still bleeding, Nelly, at this very moment. I'm bleeding myself to death."

I don't believe her. Directly I told her so. Flinging off her fat arms, which had encircled me while she spoke, with my elbows and pushing against her thigh, which she'd plumped beside me on the settle, with my knee, I shouted, "I don't ask for your pity and I don't believe you, you liar!"

Even after I read the verses in Leviticus between the checks she made with graphite pencil in the family Bible she fetched from my father's library and placed open on the settle beside me as, leaving her ironing, she admitted Kenneth, who was

[84]

late for his daily visit to my father, I didn't believe her. Afterward, I removed the checks she had made in the margin of the Bible with a rubber lead-eater.

I still don't believe her.

What I did then was gather the soiled sheet from my bed and my bloody drawers and the berry-stained apron, now smelling of lavender from having lain crumpled these days in the bottom of the press, and carry them to the shed beside the pump and plunge them into a copper kettle I filled with scalding water and beat them with a flail and scour them on a washboard with soft-soap and Fuller's earth and douse and rub and soak them in a bucking-basket filled with rainwater and bleaching power.

The sheet and the drawers came white. The purple stain in the apron, bleached to the lavender of loosestrife, stubbornly remained in the cloth.

I also tucked a napkin under my drawers, between my legs, against my bleeding crevice. And changed it four or five times daily. As Nelly assured me women do. Whether I believe her about the bleeding of other women, herself included, I can't decide.

Next day the headache was gone. And I felt scarcely any gripping in my innards. Though the bleeding continued night and day.

OCTOBER 3, 1777

The seizures stopped completely on the fourth day.

Today, the sixth, when I awoke there was no more bleeding. As Nelly had predicted. Still I don't believe her.

I don't believe her because I know what she doesn't: it wasn't God who caused *my* bleeding.

Who wounded me there I'll die before I tell her. Or anyone else.

My father slightly improves.

[85]

OCTOBER 25, 1777

A week has passed since my father rose from his bed. Joseph, muttering "whoom he luveth he chaisteneth" and such stuff, got on one side of him; Heathcliff, who stood almost as tall as my father, so much had he grown and so diminished was my father, got on the other. Between them they half-walked, half-carried him down the stairs to his place in the chimney corner of the sitting room. On his wasted frame his shirt and trousers hung as they would on the sticks of a scarecrow. His face was a skull covered with stretched parchment with holes cut in it for the glowing coals of his eyes.

Yet Kenneth assured us he had ridden out the storm. He saw no reason that in time and with care his patient should not continue to gain strength and to put flesh back on his bones. Now my father was taking nourishment from sago and arrowroot gruel and mild cheese and milk. The evening before he left his bed he had even consumed a cantlet of Nelly's cold custard pudding, a morsel of spice cake, and a half cup of negus. I thought in prospect of the time he would ask for mutton chops, his favorite meat. The danger, Kenneth warned, was another of those enervating seasonal colds. So even before winter set in I was looking forward to spring. After his descent to the sitting room, my father did show himself to be improved in spirit. Each time he took brandy and water he seemed to respond with some vigor.

With my father still unable to concern himself about the household, Joseph took immediate advantage by playing the tyrant in exercising authority over Heathcliff. Separated from me because I still had to spend long periods in my father's presence, Heathcliff found no reason to rebel or to resist Joseph's dragooning him for farm work. What with my father's ghostly transformation and the consequential daily severance of Heathcliff and me, I felt myself cut off from the world of the moors and the crags and the gorge with its waterfall and the sky and the sun and the clouds and the wind and the rain. Cribbed as I was within walls, I seemed to be living in a dream.

[86]

Even evenings, when the household would assemble in the sitting room—my father in the chimney corner, Joseph in a heavy black horsehair chair, his huge old Bible open on his lap as a desk on which he laid and counted the grimy banknotes he'd collected from the tenants, Nelly in a high-back green chair, doing needle-drudgery or netting a purse, Heathcliff and I lying on the floor in front of the fireplace—nothing seemed real. So substantial and familiar a piece of furniture as the delf-case, a huge oak dresser, with its collection of pewter dishes and glazed earthenware and china and silver mugs and tankards, or the immense old chimney piece, of carved oak, painted black, seemed to exist merely as objects described in romances exist—only so long as you are reading the words or are able to continue to imagine them after your eye has left the page. I had the feeling that should I cease to will their being, in order to keep my father alive, the old guns and horse pistols hanging above the chimney, the fireplace with its crackling peat and coal fire, the ragbag from which Nelly would pull a piece of goods to stitch into the quilt she worked on by skips, the smooth white stones I stretched on beside Heathcliff, the very house itself, all would turn to air and like clouds when the weather is changing be blown clear out of existence.

Nelly, who ordinarily moved her tongue as fast as her fingers at their work, remained strangely silent these evenings. It was not merely that she was weary from her day's tasks, I felt certain. With a hale constitution and a vast supply of strength, Nelly always had energy in reserve in the evening for prattle. It was rather as if the ebb of my father's and her father's life had caused a sinking of her spirit. Her abdication as mistress of gossip provided Joseph the opportunity to preside with his vinegar tongue. Convincing himself as he did that every soul save his own was heading directly for fire and brimstone, he was ever ready with proof-text and sermon. Now he openly interpreted my father's being smitten as a judgment and punishment upon the household for its iniquity. He took it upon himself to point his long moral finger at Nelly and Heathcliff and me, letting the greatest burden of guilt fall upon me, since, cunning hypocrite that he was, he recognized the risk he ran by too directly arraigning Nelly and Heathcliff, my father's favorites.

I put no stock in Joseph's indictments. The sins he attributed to me were to my mind of no account: sloth, lack of respect for and outright disobedience to God and to him, neglect of prayer, failure to read Scripture and pious tomes and tracts, leading myself astray by being attracted to the Devil's filth, by which he meant any secular book, singing heathen songs and ballads, being lighthearted. Of the guilt I actually experienced, a guilt so weighty as to be beyond any lifting by pious observances and so hard as to be beyond any melting by religious sentiments and so piercing as to cause the shedding of blood, Joseph had no notion.

Living with that guilt as I had now for weeks, I had struggled to comprehend it, convinced as I was of its far reach and its unpardonable nature. I could make nothing of it. For the joining of myself to Heathcliff seemed anything but sinful. Indeed, it was proper and necessary, since in spirit already we were one. Although we never spoke to each other of our kindredness—living it, there was no need to—we knew; and we knew that the other knew that whatever of joy or anguish, whatever of desire or satiety, whatever of excitement or ennui, whatever of hope or dread, whatever of necessity or chance, whatever throbbing of the heart or transport of the nerves or quickening of the blood one of us experienced, likewise did the other. Our souls were fed by the same water. Our bodies were invigorated by the same flowing sap. Our conjunction was elemental and therefore lay beyond question or qualification or judgment. Not mere communication we enjoyed; we communed. That any sundering diminished the life of both so that our separate existences thinned to dream was proof enough. Being for us was cleaving one to the other. Anything less was mere endurance.

Joined so in spirit, beyond our choice or even our will, we had come to unite our flesh in the most natural and seemingly innocent ways: first upper to nether, as Hindley and Nelly had instructed us by example, then the more nearly perfect union of both of our nether parts, our vitals, a fulfillment we had discovered for ourselves. The first of these our practices or rites had brought us naught but pleasure, yes, joy, as it ought. The second, in its greater degree of completeness, its near absoluteness of cleaving, should have transported us into a commensurate state of ecstasy. Instead, whatever momentary rapture it had effected, it had also visited upon us pain and blood. Why, my soul cried out, when we were one in spirit, created of common breath and made to breathe as one in this our life, why should the cleaving of our flesh be not just sin but sin contaminating and unpardonable? Yet that it was indeed so I could no more deny or hedge than I could the selfsameness of our spirits. Although the words of Scripture, engrained in my mind since early childhood, would seem to be my accuser, it was not the authority of the Bible, by which Joseph damned others and claimed salvation for himself, that struck me with guilt. It was the blood—first my own, then my father's, then my own again. The blood was the living judgment.

If I paid no heed to the pharisaical indictments and condemnations that issued from Joseph's sour mouth those evenings in the sitting room, neither did Heathcliff. Of that I could be certain. For her part, however, Nelly, whose tongue ordinarily was as quick and as sharp to reply to attack as were the claws of a cat, permitted Joseph to rail at her, as every so often he dared, or slyly and covertly to snipe at her, tiring of me and even of Heathcliff as his victim, I supposed because we ignored him. As was her silence, Nelly's tolerance was occasioned by more than weariness and boredom. That sagging spirit I detected allowed Joseph's words, barbed as they were, to sink into her softness without appearing to cause her to feel so much as a pinprick.

Finding that his Apollyon-like fusillades of darts either missed their marks completely or were unable to penetrate to the quick of their targets, Joseph then turned his jaundiced eye and venom-spitting tongue upon my father. Directly he advised him that the bow of God's wrath was bent and that the arrow of eternal punishment aimed unerringly at his heart. To support his cruel contentions, he croaked out the most

[89]

diabolical passages of Scripture he had been able to find by rummaging and ransacking his Bible for scores of years. The sitting room seethed with Hell, Tophet, Gehenna, the bottomless pit, abysses, brimstone, burning pitch, lakes of fire, flaming swords, snares, horrible tempests, hailstones, pestilence. The wainscot blistered, the fireplace seethed, the ceiling reeked, the stones oozed pollution. Not only did my father refrain from reprimanding Joseph or turning his remonstrances and admonitions aside; he seemed more than content to listen, indeed appeared to solicit Joseph's Jeremiah-like lamentations and reproaches and warnings of doom.

Finally, the evening before last I could endure the old hypocrite's disrespect toward my ailing father no longer. He had just read from his huge Bible that verse from one of the prophets, "for they have sown the wind, and they shall reap the whirlwind; it hath no stalk; the bud shall yield no meal: if so be it yield, the strangers shall swallow it up," and was applying its condemnation with particularity and vigor to my father, Hindley, and me, the house of Earnshaw. Then with a positively Satanic glee he craunched, "Ech, maister, ye have sown th' wind and nu ye maun reap th' whorlwind."

"Insolent old man," I cried, springing to my hands and knees as within my flesh I felt a couched cat ready to spring on an enemy, "you shall not talk to my father thus!"

Rather than welcome my intervention on his behalf, my father with more energy than I had seen him manifest since he had been felled by the hemorrhage, rose to Joseph's defense.

"Nay, Cathy," he declared sternly, "thou are a froward child. I cannot love thee; thou are worse than thy errant brother. Best say thy prayers and beseech God's pardon. I doubt thy mother and I must rue we ever reared thee!"

This reprimand not only effectually silenced me; it cut me to the quick. Joseph poured salt on the wound by clucking his currant-colored tongue and gabbling about two she-bears coming forth from the wood and tearing wicked and offald bairns to pieces. I had to bite my lip.

If during his convalescence my father heartlessly rejected my good intentions toward him and sharply rebuked me, and if he indeed welcomed and condoned Joseph's tale-bearing and inculpating and doomsaying, even when touched in his own person, and if he manifested his fondness for Nelly by remarking many a time and oft how she was a "cant lass" or a "bonny miss," or a "fess and comely maid," he absolutely doted and fawned upon Heathcliff. So highly did he sing Heathcliff's praises that in time Joseph was forced to exclude Heathcliff from his arraignments and imprecations, except for his use of the most subtle and furtive means, which policy meant, of course, that Nelly and especially I came in for even more of his reprobations. My father would ever have Heathcliff, as he lay on the floor of the sitting room, close to where he sat by the chimney, so that he might press one or the other of his bony legs against Heathcliff's back or side. And a dozen times of an hour he leaned forward and ran his clawlike fingers through the tangle of Heathcliff's black hair or stroked his forehead or cheek. Almost it seemed he needed something that was within Heathcliff, which, since Heathcliff never responded to his adulation and caressing by a word or look or gesture, only his hand laid upon Heathcliff's flesh could secure for him.

That need was insatiable. As close as I felt to Heathcliff, as much as we were one in spirit, I now found myself unable to share in and be gratified by my father's manifest love for him. Indeed, jealousy so raged in me that at such moments I hated Heathcliff. With bitterness I resented his allowing my father to touch and fondle and use him, when except for me he would never permit anyone else, not even Nelly, to demonstrate any affection for him. And yet even my jealous passion, aroused by a two-sided envy and wicked as it was, ultimately strengthened the bonding of Heathcliff's and my spirits. If I enjoyed any consolation, it was to remind myself of what I knew so absolutely as to brook no doubt: that should I deign to ask "nay" of Heathcliff when my father pleaded "yea," "nay" would be it. It even crossed my mind that my father himself sensed that whatever of affection Heathcliff would accept from him, whatever claims of generosity, kindness, and love he might set forth, Heathcliff's final allegiance was to me. I

[91]

wondered, therefore, whether my sovereignty over Heathcliff, even though I refrained from exercising it, might qualify my father's affection for me.

Last evening we were thus assembled in the sitting room. Although the day had been warm for so deep into autumn, a vigorous breeze had sprung up in late afternoon. By teatime the sky looked wild and stormy. As I lay on the floor beside Heathcliff, while Nelly fettled up the tea things, then returned and arranged her work upon her lap, I listened to the wind blustering through the firs and thorn trees outside and roaring down the chimney. I had taken only a swallow of tea and milk, for I had awakened in the morning with not a headache but a twinge between my eyes that made me sense a headache in the offing, also with a bit of queerness in my stomach. All day a malaise had oppressed me. That and the smarting of soul over the charged and crossed emotions in the household made me tolerate in determined silence the viciousness of Joseph. Indeed, I was somewhat cheered to see my father well enough to nibble a biscuit spread with marmalade while he sipped his tea.

Feeling rather too warm lying flat with my face toward the fire, I scooted to one side of the chimney, my father's not Joseph's side, and sat up, stretching my legs out in front of me. Heathcliff thereupon rolled over and laid his head in my lap. In order to secure support for my back, which ached a bit in the lower portion, I scuttled closer to my father's seat and leaned against his knee. All at once I felt his skeletal fingers riffling my hair. My suppose was that, half dozing, he had not noticed it was I who rested against him and thus imagined it was Heathcliff's hair he was fondling. But to my great surprise and even greater joy, it turned out that he had willed to caress his daughter.

"Why canst thou not always be a good lass, Cathy?" he suddenly asked.

The implication of his question almost simultaneously contaminated for me whatever affection I had for a split instant realized that he was bestowing. A flash of disappointed fury lit up in my mind his fathering of Nelly out of wedlock. Before I was able to prevent my saucy tongue, I had blurted out in reply, "Why cannot you always be a good man, Father?"

I felt his hand drop from my hair. A pang of pain shot through my heart. Taking my eyes from the thick-ribbed stockings of Joseph, exposed between the tops of his hobnail boots and the bottoms of his hiked-up trousers, at which I had been staring with disgust, and turning my head, I gazed into my father's face. Those pointed words of mine, uttered so tetchily, had affected it as had the wind in the afternoon the clear blue sky. It became darkly, heavily beclouded. The spot in the bottom of the left irid burned luridly.

Quickly I snatched his hand and kissed it, then twined our fingers. It was like holding hands with five twigs on the end of an oak branch in the dead of winter. In order to pacify and lull and woo him, I began to sing in a very soft voice, "The Bonnie House of Airlie," a ballad I knew he was fond of. Slowly his strengthless fingers slipped from mine and his head sank so that his chin rested on his breast.

"Hush," Nelly whispered. "He's fallen asleep. Don't stir for fear of waking him."

I let my voice trail off in the middle of a verse. For a space we sat in silence, hearing between the hoarse ralings of the wind the crackle of the fire and the ticking of the clock on the landing of the staircase and the click of snuffers as Nelly laid aside her work and removed a burnt wick from the oil lamp on the table beside her. The flames of the lamp and the candles fluttered, making the shadows on the walls and ceilings dance weirdly. Suddenly the clock chimed nine.

Joseph was the first to stir.

"Aye," he groaned, clapping his Bible closed, "aw mun wake th' maister for prayers an' bed."

When my father didn't respond to Joseph's words, the old man came shambling across the floor and, reaching over Heathcliff and me, shook my father by the shoulders. Then snatching the candle from the mantle, he held it under my father's eyes, which I could see were closed in his drooping

[93]

head. Replacing the candle, Joseph reached down and seized Heathcliff and me each by an arm and squeezing with his powerful fingers lifted us to our feet.

"Frame upsteers," he whispered hoarsely, "clear off t' yahr beds an' maik scant din. Yah mich praïy by yahrseln 'tis eevin'. Aw hev summut tuh doo."

"I shall bid Father goodnight first," I declared defiantly. And wrenching myself from Joseph's grip, viselike as it was, I threw my arms around my father's neck. His skin felt cool and damp as the stone of the fairy cave at the bottom of Penistone Crags. As I went rearing off in horror, he came falling forward against me. Joseph caught him and shunting me aside carried him back into the chimney seat.

"Oh, he's dead, Heathcliff!" I screamed. "He's dead!" And flinging myself onto Heathcliff I began to sob. Although I felt him shudder, no sound came from his lips. Nelly, however, commenced an unearthly wail.

Joseph seized the occcasion to sermonize.

"Ech, whet muh yuh be thinkin' uf," he croaked, "t' set up sich a heeth'nish roar uver a saint that's goan tuh Hevin. Wisht, wumin, skift. Fetch Kinnith an' th' pairsen fruh Gimmerton."

Stifling her cries, though tears streamed down her cheeks, Nelly scurried over to my father. Although his eyes were closed as if he were sleeping, she pressed her thumbs on the lids. He never stirred. Then snatching a cloak that hung on the back of the open door to the peat store, she went scurrying out into the night.

Quickly stepping around Joseph, Heathcliff grabbed me by the hand and led me, still sobbing, up the staircase at a run. We darted into our chamber. Since ours was a children's bedroom, there was no bolt to be drawn on the inside, only one on the outside to lock us in when we were being confined for misbehavior. Heathcliff left the door slightly ajar, the better to hear approaching footsteps.

"If Joseph chivvies us here," Heathcliff muttered through his teeth, "we'll crawl out through the casement and climb

[94]

down the fir tree. We can stay the night in the loft of the barn and be warm."

I agreed through tears and sobs. Not even by clamping my teeth on my tongue could I stop. It was the first time I had ever let Heathcliff see me cry.

Positioning ourselves just inside the door, we squatted hearkening until the clock struck half past nine, ready to scamper through the open panels of my oak-case bed, where Heathcliff had unhasped the window in the event we should have to open it hurriedly. I listened to the howl of the wind as it drove against the other side of the house.

Hearing no sound below, we concluded that Joseph was conducting a watch of silent Scripture and prayer in the chamber where his dead master sat. *My* father, I knew, was no longer there. Nor was Nelly's.

"Were I dead, I'd rather have a demon watch over me," Heathcliff growled.

When Heathcliff entered me last night, after my father died, I felt almost none of the pain I had experienced in the dimple of the slade. I never hesitated as, swollen and hard as a green squash, he approached me. Already we had committed the unpardonable sin together. Being beyond forgiveness is an absolute state. Like perfection. Nothing can be taken away. Or added. At least we existed in that condition *together*.

While my father was still alive after having been stricken, never would I have dared again. Even though, along with Heathcliff, already I was beyond salvation, I could have brought additional calamity upon my father. But now he was untouchable. And I, though damned, was free.

Although I had just become fully an orphan, cleaving with Heathcliff I felt complete. As our bodies joined, we intertwined. Our single soul wrapped itself around itself. Together we comprised the universe.

If one part of me did experience a few twinges of pain, so remote was that feeling that it seemed it was happening to somebody else. I, the true I, the deepest I, I whole, I was

[95]

suffused with ecstasy, of which the pain was only a peripheral part. Because I was not only Catherine Earnshaw; I was also Heathcliff. And Heathcliff was I, Catherine Earnshaw. The spirit of the water of the branch that was Catherine Earnshaw and the spirit of the water of the branch that was Heathcliff momently had drifted back into the single stream from which they had come; the living substance, the sap, of the limb that was Catherine Earnshaw and the living substance of the limb that was Heathcliff, for the nonce, had oozed back into the trunk out of which both limbs had issued. One spirit, one body.

———————

Time without measure.

Though the door of our chamber remained ajar, I heard no striking of the clock on the landing of the stairwell. How our bodies at last fell apart, I cannot say. But suddenly I experienced a wrenching and ripping of the spirit; I felt as if I were half a tree being torn asunder by some diabolically powerful force.

Heathcliff, it seems, had landed back in the world of separate beings with distinct bodies more quickly than had I.

"Haste!" he whispered, "it's Nelly."

After tossing me my frock, he went diving into his pantaloons and yanked on his smock. There was not time to close the door, for Nelly's heavy footstep was already at the top of the stairs. I had only a moment in which to string on my apron, without doing the hooks and eyes of my frock, over my naked limbs before Nelly's candle threw its light down the hallway. Heathcliff had enough command to seat me on the side of my cabinet bed, where the panels stood open, while he leaped onto the foot of his trestle bed across the room from me. Behind her wavering candle Nelly came toddling through the door.

"Be comforted, Cathy," Heathcliff murmured, "by the thought that already he's heard the trumpet blow at the Eastern Gate."

"Where God shall wipe away all tears from his eye; and there shall be no more death, neither sorrow, nor crying, neither shall there be any more pain," I had the presence of mind to reply, falling back on paraphrase of familiar Scripture.

"Ah, you sweet young souls," Nelly gasped, "still awake and comforting each other." And placing her candle on the three-legged table beside the trunk with the iron hoops, she broke into sobs as she gathered us into her arms, an aunt solacing two orphaned children.

I listened for the wind, but it had died.

OCTOBER 30, 1777

This day saw my spirit descend to the lowest depth ever in this my life. Only absolute separation from Heathcliff could plunge me any lower. That indeed would be to be cast into the bottomless pit. This day was the day of my father's burial.

I awoke with that hand squeezing my innards. And the megrim. When I slid apart the panels of the oak cabinet and stepped onto the floor of the chamber, once more the room went spinning about me. In the gray light of dawn, I could see that again I had bled the bed. Not to put stock in what Nelly had told me was right. Here was fresh proof that Heathcliff, not God, was cause of my issue of blood. His inhabiting me three nights ago had abraded the old wound in my crevice and now it had broken open a second time and the blood was flowing.

Again I used the napkin, as Nelly had instructed me, despite the difference in author from what she had insisted. I had to drag myself like a beaten hound through my waking hours.

I have a new sister. Hindley returned to the Heights the day before yesterday, fetched hither by my father's death and imminent interment. To our utter surprise he brought with him a wife. Where and how he had acquired her, God alone knows, for he offered no explanation. My father, I am convinced, died without having learned that his son had married. Whether Hindley deigned not to inform him out of scantness of filial affection and respect, or whether he dared not out of fear of being cut off, I can't determine.

Hindley's introduction of his bride into the household has led Nelly to turn to me as confidante. I am neither pleased nor flattered. Presently she lacks power to keep her feelings to herself, for it is evident that she is driven nigh insane with jealousy. And the truth is there is no one but me to whom she can unburden herself on such a matter.

To her old lover Hindley she is curt, cold, and correct. In waiting on his spouse, Frances, she permits her disdain to show and allows herself to be as sullen and surly as she can without letting herself be charged with such conduct. Hindley, knowing of course the cause of her pique, proves anxious not to risk provoking her by venturing a rebuke, even though Nelly points her sallies to hurt. They also frighten Hindley by threatening more.

Over tea the evening of Hindley's arrival, Frances in all innocence declared to Nelly her hankering after being introduced to the country where her new husband had been born and bred. Hindley himself was absent, having gone to Gimmerton to make arrangements with the rector and the joiner, who also serves as embalmer and undertaker.

"Well," Nelly replied, "you must know that our winters here are lengthy and oppressive. The wind strikes fierce; it batters us even in summer. Severe storms regularly rattle and shake us. Our air is thin and, for weak constitutions"—here she threw Frances a lingering, deliberate look—"perilous. The sun, when it appears, slants in across our hills, casting long shadows. Our slopes are steep and rocky. Stone, gray-black stone lies on every hand. Our villages are small and remote, our farms sparsely scattered; our footpaths are narrow and difficult of access. We are a hard and hardy race, who keep to ourselves and look inward. On those who are foreign to our parts we look with suspicion and hostility."

The poor target of this attack either has so little wit that she failed to realize that she was being hectored, or else her spirit is so mean that she was unable to resent it. Were I to be so

[98]

treated, my teeth would bare and my claws would out, I can assure you.

In private to me Nelly rails continually against the woman she imagines to be a successful rival.

"Even before he has been laid in the ground, your father must be writhing inside his coffin. Little as he professed to think of Hindley, he did, I am certain, nourish secret hopes of him. And believed that married to a firm-willed, strong-minded woman he might become a respectable gentleman farmer of the north. And to have him wed to such a chit, bringing her here to present to us on the occasion of his father's funeral! Why she even lacks the breeding that would indicate that despite her silliness and stupidity she brought her husband a name and something more. I daresay she gives the appearance of being some small merchant's or shopkeeper's bantling."

Being aware of Nelly's origin, as I was, I was tempted to laugh in her face. But I must confess that my knowing without Nelly's knowing that I knew and without my knowing whether Nelly herself knew was making me uncomfortable. Yet I thought Nelly ought not be so full of spite and venom. When it comes to traversing a precarious path in safety, avoiding the quicksand of having to swallow her feelings and also avoiding the rock of having to pay the price of outright insolence, Nelly is a sure-footed pioneer.

As much as I deplore Nelly's barbarous attacks on Frances and refuse though I do to join Nelly in her behind-the-back maligning, as she invites me to, I approve Hindley's choice of a wife no more than she does. Frances is eiderdown covered with silk shaped like a butterfly. So narrow is her waist I believe my thumbs and forefingers might span it. Her tiny feet are neither substantial enough to romp the moors nor arched sufficiently for that water whose passage bespeaks gentility to run beneath her instep without wetting. So tiny and soft her hands that they can be good for nothing but hooking eyes and tying sashes and ribands and fixing curlpapers. Her hemp-colored hair she wears behind, fastened with a Spanish comb. Above her short upper lip, which is thick and has a deep indentation, her nose is snub. Between her lower lip, which protrudes and pouts, forming her mouth into a little cup, and her round-as-a-knob-on-a-newel chin is another deep indentation. Her forehead is shallow, her vacant dun-colored eyes set so far apart they seem not to belong to each other, her cheeks beneath them flat. There are dimples in her whey-face. Undoubtedly she has what passes for prettiness in a dandy's eyes. But to my mind it is a prettiness that bespeaks simple-mindedness when she is pleased, and petulance when she is crossed.

In manner she is careless, never listening but always chattering on about the most barmy stuff. And she is full of vagaries. With my father lying there in his coffin, she refuses to step into the sitting room, passes the doorway skittishly, with her skirts held up and her face averted, as if death were a mouse. She openly avows that she dreads wearing black and confesses that when her mother died she was too frightened of its effects to put on her finger a mourning ring. Such cowardly superstitiousness revolts me. When she flutters her cambric handkerchief with a lace border, then titters into it, it is impossible to know whether she is giggling or whimpering. She lisps and her tongue slights the consonants and favors the vowels of her speech. All feathers and paduasoy, without a particle of iron in her soul, she would ignite and incinerate from one flash of inner fire. I find her lighter than vanity.

So changed in his person is my brother Hindley that I doubt I should have known him away from the Heights. Although he has not grown tall—indeed, Heathcliff now stands within a few inches of him—he seems to have acquired height because he has become so spare, losing all of the plumpness of my mother's that formerly sat on his small frame. And the ruddy color has disappeared from his cheeks. He dresses himself like a gentleman from town—in a satin doublet and an embroidered waistcoat, his breeches tucked into highly polished Hessians. He looks absurd. His way of speaking has changed into the mincing manner of his wife, on whom he conspicuously dotes. After breakfast this morning, when she opened the sluicegates of her eyes and uttered gasping little protests, he assured her that, the day being windy and cold and she being delicate, her remaining at home rather than accompanying the father-in-law she had never seen to the kirkyard with the rest of the household would not be scandalous. Nelly is right. My brother does have deficiencies and weaknesses that easily become faults. But he also has some quality of mind and of spirit. The poppet he has married will never inspire or provoke him to exhibit either.

Overhead the sky was mottled; along the horizon, brindled, sagging so low and close that it seemed we would walk into it and bump our heads. Although I had gone to bed under a full moon, the color of a plum, during the night the first heavy snow of the season had filled the ruts dug by the cart wheels in the muddy road. Where it had drifted, for the wind was sweeping, snow rose to the height of the hips and haws of the rose and hawthorn hedge bank. In low and exposed places along the way it clogged the wheels of the hearse and balled the feet of the bayard that drayed my father's coffin toward the Gimmerton kirkyard. A number of times the six hands who were to bear the bier to the grave were required to come, some along the side of and some behind the undertaker's wagon, and heave.

As our curtal procession crossed the humpbacked bridge over the beck, just before the descent into the hollow in which the village lies, my eyes swept the moorlands around us: the snow toned purple on the dale heads, where earth and sky touched; blue in the middle distance, the wold and the coombes; white in the low fields and meadows. Already many of the trees along the road were bare-limbed. Snow weighed down the branches of the hemlocks, larches, and cedars.

Although the keen air cleared my head, my innards were stretched taut. Every so often the hand in there would tug on those strings so it wrenched me. Disapprove as I did of my brother, revolted as I was by the conduct of his bride, grieving as I was for my father, my self-concern dwarfed these feelings. Frightened by the recommencing of the issue of blood, wondering if and when the wound would heal and the flow

[101]

would cease, as it had before, I took solace only in the presence of Heathcliff, even though he and I were not alone.

In accordance with Hindley's instructions, only the inner household and the six pall-bearing hands were to attend the service for the dead the rector would conduct in the graveyard. Not even Shielders or Kenneth was included. Nor the head of the only other genteel family close by, Mr. Linton of Thrushcross Grange. To my eye Nelly's mother was conspicuously absent. Upon our return from the kirkyard, the house would be opened to the handful of neighbors and the few village gossips who wished to show their respect for the ancient family by mourning in the customary way. Because of her nerves and because the occasion scarcely seemed propitious for introducing his bride to the neighborhood, Frances might remain upstairs, Hindley had declared, until the mourners departed.

As we approached the graveyard, situated on the fringe of the village, I could see a mound of whitened mools, which told me that a hole its size had been dug beside it. Nearby stood the sexton and a helping delver, leaning on their long-handled spades, waiting to undo what recently they had done to the earth. What with the spate of rain we had had and the season's not being far enough advanced toward cold for more than surface frost, digging must needs have been easy.

Between two fir trees that grew at the head of the yawning black hole in the sod, their lower branches sweeping along the ground like full skirts under their load of snow, stood the rector, wrapped in his greatcoat, a scarf muffling his throat, gaiters protecting his spindly legs, as he intoned beneath his shovel hat. Hindley, in a surtout and a beaver hat, positioned himself at the foot of the grave.

Between the white-covered mound of mould and the edge of the grave along one side, stood Joseph, in his black Sunday garb, his round John Knox hat jammed onto his rime-frost hair, and Heathcliff, bare-headed, his dark locks tossing in the wind, dressed in the black jupe Hindley had mourned our mother in, already skimpy on his tall broad frame. Along the

[102]

other side of the grave Nelly and I stood, Nelly wearing a gown from the period of mourning for my mother and over it a cloak and a hood of hodden gray, against the wind and the cold, I wearing a black merino mourning frock and chemisette Hindley and Frances had brought for me, with a black mantel thrown over my shoulders. In the pocket of my frock was a pair of black leather gloves I refused to wear. My hair was pulled in under a simple cottage bonnet, which served as a mourning cap. While my eye took to roaming the hillside, its face lined with gray stone walls, beyond the farthest edge of the kirkyard, my ear, refusing to distinguish into words the cant the rector was snuffling, tuned to the soughing and sighing of wind, which I imagined my father's breath had joined.

The rector commenced the closing prayer, commending the soul of my father to Heaven. All heads, even the hands' and the sexton's and his helper's, all save Heathcliff's and mine, were bowed. In this, the old section of the graveyard, close by the kirk, some of the thickly sewn headstones were flat, but the preponderance of them were upright slabs inclining every which way. The horizontal stones were white with snow, like tables covered with linen, the vertical dark and glistening from the snow which had them wet without itself adhering to them. Wandering, my eye lighted on a large headstone set perpendicular, just behind where Heathcliff stood. In contrast to the grim gray and black stone elsewhere, this stone was honey-colored. Even in the densely overcast light it shone like the top of Penistone Crags under a bright sun. So close to it was Heathcliff that his legs and feet in deep shadow before it seemed to be invisible; for an instant I had the illusion that he was kneeling with his back to a golden tapestry of Berlin wool. Either the grave over which the stone presided was the extreme portion of our family's plot division or it was the closest ground of our nearest kirkyard neighbor.

When the rector intoned "A-men," Hindley went striding off immediately, followed by the rector, then Joseph, then Heathcliff. I lingered, staring at the honey-colored stone, until I heard the first clods thump on the lid of my father's walnut coffin. Sensing that Nelly was not accompanying me, I looked around. She was handing his spade back to the sexton.

"Come, child," she murmured, gently taking me by the elbow as she caught up with me. While we walked on behind Joseph and Heathcliff, I eased my arm from her grip, in order to stop and read the inscription on the honey-colored headstone, around the base of which frost-blasted nettles and withered dock leaves and sere blades of grass protruded from the snow. What I read sent a stitch through my heart:

HEATHCLIFF EARNSHAW
b. July 24, 1754
d. December 24, 1756
The firstborn of thy sons shalt thou give.

I stood for an instant, swaying with bewilderment. Then I began to phrase to myself questions which the inscription propounded but which I, being so far from able to answer, could make no sense of. How could Heathcliff, who was alive, walking this instant on the snowy road beside Joseph, lie underneath that headstone? How could Heathcliff, when he was not my father's and mother's child, be named "Earnshaw"? How could Heathcliff, who was but a year older than I, be born and die before Hindley was born? My head, around which the kitchen had stopped spinning during breakfast, now felt the kirkyard whirling about it.

Dizzily I ran after Nelly.

"Nelly," I called breathlessly, then catching her, seized the edge of her cloak, which the gale was causing to flap about her. "I must show you something. Over here." My voice sounded birdlike, faraway, strange to my ears.

"What is it, Catherine?" she asked. "We ought not dawdle in the cold and wind."

By the hand I led her back to the headstone. While she took in what I pointed to, I kept my eyes fixed on her face, aimed them at the little dull fleck in the bottom of her left irid. Fingers inside me were tying the string around the bottom of my stomach into knot after knot. I felt they could never be untangled.

"Oh," she sighed. Then went on. "Did your father never tell you?" From the tone of her voice and the expression on her face I could not ascertain whether she was genuinely offhand or was acting so in order to conceal her perplexity. In the hope her touch might be more revealing I tightened my grip on her hand.

"Tell me what?" I demanded.

"That there was a child who died. Before Hindley or you were born. A son."

"Neither my father nor my mother ever mentioned such a child."

Nelly sighed again. "Ah. I suppose your mother considered you too young to be bothered about such a grievous affliction of the family. And it must be that after your mother's departure, untimely as it was, your father concluded there was no reason further to darken your already clouded life with another tale of sorrow."

I could judge nothing more from Nelly's hand in mine than that my own blood was racing furiously.

"Then Hindley is not my only brother."

"Surely he is your only living brother."

"Is Hindley aware that he is not firstborn?"

"That you must ask him."

"But how do you know about this thing?"

"Catherine, Catherine, this is no time for an inquisition into these old affairs. You'll catch your death out here in the wintery blast. And I will, too."

With that pronouncement she attempted to wrest her hand free of mine. I clapped my other hand upon hers, imprisoned it, clutched it as though I were drowning.

"Nelly, I must know."

"Well, though the poor little thing lived and died before my time, I, being so much older than you and closer to that period, always knew, I suppose. I may have overheard laments. The death of his firstborn son was indeed a grievous blow and occasioned much grief to your father, I'm certain.

[105]

And, of course, my mother having lived nearby all her life would know. In fact, now that I put my mind on it, I seem to remember having heard that my mother tended the poor little lamb, just as she did Hindley."

I felt my breathing shorten. Still I kept her hand tight-clasped, and I riveted my eyes on that little dark spot in her left irid.

"Why should Heathcliff, who is no kin of mine, bear the name of my dead brother?"

Uttering his name made me see with my inner eye the already tall, broad-shouldered figure of Heathcliff, made me see his swarthy skin, his curly locks of black hair, his cavernous black eyes with their ever-present glisten, made me see him though he and Joseph had disappeared in the road behind the hedge bank and though I kept my outer eye fastened on that little wem in Nelly's eye.

"Your father had him so christened because when he was brought to the Heights the sad abandoned creature could not give himself a name. Now you've heard all how and about it, missy. I'll answer no more of your idle questions. And on this day we have laid your father in the earth, I'd advise you to think only on his goodness and kindness to you, for he was a generous man and the best of fathers, and not to worrit and moider yourself after a brother you never knew. Every father has some sorrow he keeps from his children for fear of troubling them. Come, we have miles to home."

With that, by main force she wrenched her hand free of the pincers in which I held her. And turning ripped the fleck in her eye from my gaze. Then went wending her way between the gravestones toward the road.

I dropped to my knees in the snow, my fingers grasping the weathered top of the honey-colored headstone, my dizzied head lurching forward onto my hooked fingers, my eyes falling closed. The hand inside my belly tugged the knot it was working on so savagely that I cried out, an animal roar of pain. That hand, I suddenly knew, was my father's. And then I felt myself spinning down into the vortex of the cold black pool at the bottom of Penistone Crags. Bottomless it was, I could tell. And the whirling would never stop.

While my soul descended, how long my body remained at that fateful spot in such an attitude I have no notion. The outside cold and the wind I was aware of not at all. Within were icy water and turbulence.

I felt a soft hand plump on my shoulder.

"If you wish to pray longer, my child, I beg of you do so within doors," a nasal voice admonished. "Moved as God is by grief that pays no heed to wind and weather, your silent words and thoughts will rise to His ears just as swiftly and intactly if you send them from the shelter of the church."

The demon in me howled in laughter and pain.

[3]

The Helmet of Salvation

NOVEMBER 1, 1777

Another blow. From a different quarter. A stroke that threatens to change life at the Heights externally—the habits and patterns of the household. The fact is that the free access to each other Heathcliff and I have always enjoyed now is imperiled. How fiercely our joined spirits crave the presence of each other's physical being!

This afternoon Mr. Green, the attorney from Gimmerton, appeared and closeted himself with Hindley in the sitting room. His visit, it turns out, was neither initiated by Hindley nor merely fortuitous. It seems that my father, sensing his days on earth were numbered, had summoned Green in order to draw a new will. In view of my father's demise, Green informed Nelly, he was keeping the appointment my father had made, using the opportunity to apprise my brother of the contents and terms of the will of my father that legally was in force.

Green and Hindley remained together less than an hour, the provisions of the document being straightforward and clear. After the attorney's departure Hindley assembled the inner household in the sitting room, and with Frances ensconced beside him on the horsehair sofa, so that they might counterpoint his stern address to the rest of us with their billing and cooing, he presented himself as the now master of the house and property, and Frances as mistress. I must say I find these turtledoves more loathsome than hateful. Heathcliff and I would scorn such a puling expression of our devotion.

My father, Hindley informed us, had bequeathed the entire estate to him, Hindley—the Heights, its furnishings, its lands, including tenant farms, rents, and incomes, and certain sums of hard savings and invested moneys. To the servants, as Hindley designated Nelly and Joseph, nothing was left. And from that instant, Hindley proclaimed, Nelly and Joseph were forbidden to occupy the sitting room with the family, as had been the custom within all of my memory, but were to keep to the back kitchen, thus leaving the house proper for himself and his bride.

Nor was any sum of money or portion of property settled upon me.

Hindley returned to the servants. Joseph, he decreed, should continue in his employ; his duties were to be in charge of the farmyard, to work and oversee the hands, and to collect rents and shares from the tenants. When age should render him able to toil no longer, Hindley generously assured him, he should adequately be taken care of.

Turning to Nelly, he observed that while examining Joseph's black book he had fallen upon the account of Nelly's father, who as a matter of fact had died suddenly, a little more than a month ago, not long after our visit. To his surprise he discovered that for a score of years no rent had been paid for the house he occupied, that the attached fields had been sublet and still were, and that not one farthing of the rents or a gowpen of crop from the tillage ever had been returned to the estate. Furthermore, payments of a certain sum *to* farmer Dean, which continued to be made to his widow on the last rent day, were entered. Joseph sat nodding in corroboration, muttering that he had forever been telling the master that he disapproved of such prodigal spending in that it promoted sloth. I scrutinized Nelly's face; it was set, sphinxlike.

Hindley went on to observe that he had learned from Joseph that Nelly, on the other hand, had never been paid a wage for her services at the Heights. Such irregular practices,

Hindley pronounced, peremptorily should cease. Nelly would be retained as housekeeper and as servant to the new mistress; she would draw a salary, which he was certain they should be able to agree upon, for he had no intention of treating in niggardly fashion those who continued to perform their duties faithfully; and the Widow Dean would commence paying equitable rent for the farmhouse she inhabited, which he magnanimously pledged her would not be increased so long as Nelly remained in his employ, while the customary portion of the shares from the sublet fields henceforth would be returned to the estate.

Though I knew that Hindley was acting out of partial ignorance, I could in no way forgive him for his presumptuous arrogance, his parsimony, his avarice. That already his weak nature was falling under the influence of that old reprobate and pinchpenny Joseph was clear. Although I could muster little in the way of sisterly affection for Nelly, I could not help feeling angry indignation at Hindley's callous and humiliating treatment of his former mistress, a lover I had heard him passionately insist he desired and intended to marry. Now he was turning her retroactively into his badly paid whore. I was also infuriated by his smugness and by the simpering expression of acquiescence that Frances, a foreigner who had no more notion of our household than might a Mohock Indian, felt called upon to manifest as she sat at his side on the sofa as if it were a royal seige.

That in the future I shall be spared Joseph's quarter of an hour blessing of the food and his pious harangues and Nelly's canting and threaping and snideness only means that I must endure the odiousness of Hindley and Frances.

Then Hindley fixed his eye upon Heathcliff. His own inclination, he proclaimed, was simply to turn Heathcliff out-of-doors. In no way inhibited by the thought that the poor man's body was scarce laid in the ground, he dared attack his own and my father by observing that the only way in which he ever had been able to account for Heathcliff's being permitted to remain in the household was that Heathcliff's unknown mother must have been a demon who from whatever infernal region she made her dwelling had cast a spell over the man. As if explaining away my father's great affection for Heathcliff would undo it, he made it seem that, released from this enchantment and thus no longer seeing through a glass darkly, my father would approve of his son's doing what he had himself had wished to do while on earth but had been prevented because he had been bewitched. Joseph, Hindley assured us, when consulted as an old retainer, concurred with his reasoning and seconded his determination. At which point vicious Joseph, removing his three-inch pipe, fixed his agate eye upon Heathcliff, who was sitting beside me, dropped his lantern jaw, and muttered, "Ay, theyur be fiend in th' whelp, I knew it fram . . ."

Holding up his hand to silence Joseph and to demonstrate his popelike sovereignty, Hindley went on to concede that Nelly, when advised with, had pleaded Heathcliff's case with passionate tears. As a manifestation of his desire to be generous even to so undeserving a young devil as Heathcliff, Hindley proclaimed, he had decided to allow Heathcliff temporarily and conditionally to remain at the Heights. In that he had not yet concluded what his status as a hireling with attendant duties should be, for Heathcliff was still in his nonage, he was to remain for the time under Joseph's jurisdiction. The express condition of his not being turned off was that he mend his slovenly, slothful, disrespectful, and disobedient ways by reforming himself into a smart, industrious, dutiful, and submissive servant. Sneeringly he emphasized "servant."

As I sat staring in rage at Hindley, while seeing Heathcliff only from the corner of my eye, I could not help comparing them: Hindley, neither bonny nor black, but of a complexion of dough that has not been sufficiently baked, with fine, lank, mouse-colored hair, shallow slate-colored eyes, the small bones of a cat, little teeth behind thin lips; Heathcliff swarthy, with glowing eyes in cavernous sockets, thick black locks of unruly hair, cheekbones steep as Penistone Crags, his teeth inside his fleshy lips large and white and sharp, broad-shouldered, promising to be tall. Truly, if there were much of my mother and little of my father in Hindley, there was much

[111]

of my father in Heathcliff. What kind of being, I pondered to myself, must Heathcliff's mother have been?

Dismissing Frances, Joseph, Nelly, and Heathcliff, Hindley commanded me to remain. Then in order, I suppose, to allay any suspicion I might have, or might form, of chicanery on his part, he requested that I read the will with my own eyes and thus stand satisfied. Contemptuous of his transparent motive and despising him for attributing to me the suspicion or envy he would experience were the circumstance reversed, when I care not a twitch of my little finger for all the property and money in the kingdom, save where they touch Heathcliff and me, I haughtily declined. He would not accept my refusal but kept insisting to the point at which the business was becoming tedious to me. Therefore I took up the document and perused it.

The will was written without question in my father's hand, set down on a musty piece of parchment, with the remains of the broken crimson seal on it. It was dated July 25, 1754, more than twenty-three years ago. Excluding a certain portion of my father's holdings reserved for the possession of my mother, should he precede her in death—a provision whose force, to be sure, no longer pertained—my father bequeathed all that he owned, the specifications being precisely as Hindley had reported them, to his only son.

Whether Hindley had observed what struck me almost immediately, namely, that the will had been drawn before his birth, I have no way of knowing. Had he not noticed for himself, I wondered whether Green had pointed out the fact to him. Whatever, Hindley made no observation about the date to me. For my part, I gave him no indication that I detected anything curious in that regard.

As I sat staring at the piece of parchment, I became aware that I was living an instant of crisis. I had refrained from telling Nelly what I knew for a certainty was her true parentage not merely because we were constantly tooth and nail at each other. More forceful in my enjoining myself to silence had been a desire to protect my father, her mother, Nelly herself if she did not already know and accede to the subterfuge, even the old clown who having been bought as husband for Nelly's mother had also been paid to pass as Nelly's father. That any good would eventuate from my discovery of the secret to Hindley I could not see. From his correspondence with Nelly before he had been whisked off to college, I could be certain that he had not the least suspicion that she was his half sister. And in the intervening years, I had had little opportunity to tell him even had I so chosen, for he seldom returned to the Heights and then only for spaces so brief that they discouraged any intimacy between us. To what purpose, I asked myself, now degrade my dead father in the eyes of his son while placing a burden of awful guilt, unknowing though he might have been in committing the sin, upon the son himself? Any imperative that insisted upon my revealing what I had discovered for the sake of open and full truth at the cost of pain and damage was a Levitical morality whose claim I spurned with scorn.

With regard to Nelly now, however, the case was becoming more complicated. If with my father dead she did not know whence her blood came while I did, I could not help feeling pangs of guilt for withholding such vital knowledge from her, the person most deeply affected. That my father should have died without a daughter he begot knowing that he was indeed her father struck me with horror. On the other hand, Nelly's mother, who was still among the quick, bore prime responsibility for determining what Nelly was to know and what was to be kept hidden from her. And she and my father most certainly had made a joint decision either to conceal her origin from their daughter or to make it known to her while enjoining her to secrecy. Who was *I* to gainsay her parents?

But what chiefly appalled and inhibited me was the dilemma posed by Nelly's affair with Hindley. If she had become her brother's mistress unknowingly, my disclosure of the truth would be little short of cruel, for well I now knew the pain and the guilt attendant upon that precise discovery. Dislike Nelly as I did, spat with her as I might, I harbored no feelings of vindictiveness. But the other possibility struck me as being even more ghastly, namely, that either knowing or strongly suspecting—for Nelly was shrewd, insightful, indeed sensitive with regard to intuitions almost to the point of having the second sight—Nelly still had become her own brother's lover in the flesh. With good reason I tried to dismiss the notion of such an acquiesence from my mind.

The sole pang of unqualified self-reproach I had felt in the hideous tangle was effected by my inability to share such a momentous secret with Heathcliff. Yet each time I had resolved to open myself to him, that dread which I had been unable to define had seized my will and rendered me impotent. Two days ago at the honey-colored headstone in the kirkyard that dread took definite shape.

As I had fallen whirling into the dark, the truth had flashed before my eyes like lightning. Without connecting and thus knowing, I had known enough to know. In the remote caves of my mind I had been hiding from myself the pieces I had been collecting: The physical resemblance of Heathcliff to my father. The mystery of Heathcliff's arrival, on which occasion he had issued from my father's greatcoat like a child being born, in place of the fiddle my father had promised to bring Hindley, in place of the whip I had asked for, in place of the apples and pears he had told Nelly, his third and unacknowledged child, he would bring her upon his return from that three-day visit to Liverpool whose purpose was never explained. My mother's instantaneous anger when he presented the dirty gibbering child, her hatred and persecutions of Heathcliff all her remaining days, her continued coldness to my father until her death. My father's manifest affection for Heathcliff, his preference for him over Hindley and me, even over Nelly, his oft-expressed fear of Heathcliff's mistreatment after his own death—all of which made me ask myself whether Heathcliff were truly a child of passion. The almost parallel case of Nelly. The mysterious bond between Nelly and Heathcliff, a bond that doubtlessly was forged and maintained by their recognition of their common irregular and precarious footing in the household, perhaps even by an unconscious sympathy of shared blood.

The truth did not occur to me as the result of a rationally

drawn conclusion. Nor was it gradual like the restoration of a palimpsest or learning the code to hieroglyphics. Rather, the pieces of the superimposed image slowly infiltrating my mind and being hidden in deep dark niches over a long period of time, over all the knowing years of my childhood, and lying in these recesses remote from one another, the letters HEATH-CLIFF EARNSHAW, carved into the honey-colored head-stone, had sparked the lightning which in the darkness of my fall revealed the physical form of Heathcliff fit to the figure my father had been. The dazzling radiance had blinded me like the light which had transformed Saul to Paul on the road to Damascus. Instead of ushering me into a state of grace, however, my illumination had served to reveal my corruption.

So keenly did I imagine the wretchedness my father had had to endure that now I was living that wretchedness myself.

If Nelly's craft and guardedness made it impossible for me to discover whether she knew her full parentage, I had not a grain of doubt of Heathcliff's absolute ignorance of his. Even while spinning in the dark whirlpool after my blinding, I was fearful of having to tell him. Knowing that at the center of his being, determining not only all that he did but also all that he was, was passion, the purest imaginable passion, knowing this essentialness of his because I was made of and was moved by the same passion, I had become terrified that by injecting the poisoned knowledge I had received into the purity of his passion, I might so contaminate him as to destroy him.

What is more, I realized that the consequence which necessarily would eventuate from my acting on the virulent knowledge I now unhappily possessed would threaten Heathcliff and me with unnatural and debilitating separation. I was no politic Nelly, or prudent Aeneas, able to pass unscathed through the strait between the monstrous craggy Scylla and the sucking whirlpool Charybdis. Either I must allow myself to be swallowed alone by the swirling vortex and thus be washed down her throat to oblivion, or like Odysseus I would have to reconcile myself to sacrifice some valuable and beloved parts of the company that constituted my soul to the hideous, destructive, many-handed Scylla.

[115]

That was the critical dilemma confronting me as I read and digested the significance of the date on my father's last will and testament, while sitting in the chimney corner, my father's old seat, across from Hindley on the black horsehair sofa. Neither Hindley nor Nelly should ever hear their truth from my tongue—that I had resolved. But Heathcliff . . . how could I ever seal my lips and withhold such a momentous piece of knowledge from him?

To be sure, my revelation would make no legal difference. No matter that my father's then intention in making this will could only have been to bequeath virtually all that he had to leave to his firstborn son, one Heathcliff Earnshaw, twenty-one years deceased. Or to turn the unalterable fact around, no matter that my father had never intended to bequeath all he had to a son toward whom he felt limited affection and of whose worth he was more than doubtful. Whatever the date on that will, however accidentally or ironically, Hindley alone fit the lawful designation of heir. Nor was there the least legal force to the fact that my father's intention in summoning Green for a never-to-be-kept appointment surely had been to draw a new will in which quite a different disposal of his worldly goods would have been made. How galling the difference between the moral intention of my father with regard to his favorite child, a secret illegitimate son, and the actuality of the treatment Heathcliff was being subjected to!

Assuring my brother that I was perfectly satisfied, not deigning to try to convince him that for myself the lack of provision for even the meanest dowry meant nothing—what had deeds and banknotes and stone walls and slate roofs and objects of furniture, all of which being material were extrinsic, to do with me, Catherine Earnshaw, spirit imprisoned in flesh?—I handed him the parchment and begged to be excused. Before I could be gone, Hindley drove me from disgust to outrage by affirming in the most maudlin terms and with a positively fawning manner that when it came time for me to offer myself to a proper gentleman as wife, he should see to it that I did not present myself with an empty hand. Heavy-hearted and hurting in soul, I ran from the room, up the staircase to my chamber, plunged into my oak cabinet bed, and pulled the panels closed behind me.

That Heathcliff had been commandeered by Joseph for once did not disappoint me. I could see him driving sheep past the coal shed up a plank into the barn porch for protection against the snow that had begun to fall so thick that already the ground looked like the floor of the sheepcote during shearing. For a period I needed to be alone. Although my innards suffered less from squeezing than they had earlier in the day, my head ached fearfully. I inspected myself to determine whether the wound in my crevice had commenced to heal. The blood was still issuing freely.

Now I made myself digest Hindley's pronouncements and edicts, and to face what certainly lay ahead. Nelly I had little concern about. Despite Hindley's indifference and greed, motivated by the change in the object of his affection and his own ill nature, her realism and her art would see her through. Whatever of affection or of hatred for Hindley might remain in her, I was convinced that she would not allow any such feeling to interfere with her policy. Since circumstance now dictated that she must endure some hurt and mortification in waiting on her former lover's wife, she would contrive to do so. Her revenge would be that to the limit of Hindley's perception, perhaps even of his patience, Frances should pay.

As for Nelly's mother, I had small fear that she should not be taken care of. Nelly surely would see to it that, even though Joseph's black book might show a portion of return in crops and rent, her own wages would be sufficient, over and above what she must give her mother for spending, to pay for tenancy in the farmhouse. No one needed advise Nelly that she held a double-barreled pistol at Hindley's head. Whether both those barrels were full of shot, Nelly alone knew. I could aver that one of the barrels was charged.

That Hindley meant to be not only master but tyrant, a role thrust upon him by his consciousness of his weakness, by his gnawing awareness of his limitations and deficiencies, by his apprehensions of challenges to his authority and of proofs of his will and strength by those he knows to be his superiors in both, could not be doubted. And perform before his sawney wife, present himself to her as masterful as he must, I could guess he would forgo no opportunity to play the part. Indeed, by nature he is the pink and pattern of the despot.

Of Hindley's assertion that generosity and Nelly's pleas had played a role in determining his policy toward Heathcliff, I believed not a pea's worth. His hatred of Heathcliff I knew to be implacable; his fear of him I knew to run to his very heart. As a consequence, Heathcliff's future at the Heights would be decided by naught but the outcome of the struggle between Hindley's vindictiveness and his cowardice. So long as he would be able to humiliate Heathcliff with impunity, would be able to make him suffer without danger of reprisal, he would allow Heathcliff to remain. His mean and jealous nature would be busy finding ways to cause Heathcliff increasing misery. Mortifying him in my presence, proclaiming his servitude to Joseph, which would effectively separate him from me, putting him on the rack of suspense with regard to his future at the Heights were the beginning. The instant Hindley's fear of Heathcliff overpowered his hatred, however, Heathcliff, I'd warrant, should be gone in a trice.

Plunged as I am into the Slough of Despond, beaten and bruised as I am by Giant Despair, threatened as I am by a craven Apollyon, I have a consolation and a hope. The consolation is the near certitude that my father, having been too neglectful of his affairs to alter his will from the time of the death of his firstborn, intended at the first moment he felt himself sufficiently restored after his seizure, to bequeath his estate in accordance with the dictates of his heart and his troubled conscience. Had my father lived one more day, Nelly and her mother would have found themselves with a comfortable sufficiency for the remainder of their lives—that I do believe. I am equally convinced that rather than cut off Heathcliff without a farthing and abandon him to the vengeance of Hindley, my father should have expressed his love for Heathcliff materially and answered his own fear that he be mistreated after his death. I refuse to be so weak as to

[118]

speculate about my father's intentions toward his acknowledged daughter.

My hope lies in the fact that Heathcliff and I still lodge in the same house. Thus I am provided some time to decide if and when and how I ought to tell him, am provided time without the pain of full separation, which I much fear would disable me, to consider what with my mean prospects I possibly might do to advance Heathcliff's welfare and at the same time to permit us to continue in each other's presence, interfusing our spirits. My own happiness, my own life is the forfeit.

NOVEMBER 8, 1777

An awful Sunday! I wish my father were back again. Hindley is a detestable substitute—his conduct to Heathcliff is atrocious. Heathcliff and I are going to rebel—we took our initiatory step this evening.

All day had been flooding with rain; we could not go to church, so Joseph must needs get up a congregation in the garret; and while Hindley and his wife basked downstairs before a comfortable fire, doing anything but reading their Bibles, I'll answer for it, Heathcliff, myself, and the unhappy ploughboy were commanded to take our prayerbooks and mount. We were ranged in a row, on a sack of corn, groaning and shivering, and hoping that Joseph would shiver too, so that he might give us a short homily for his own sake. A vain idea! The service lasted precisely three hours; and yet my brother had the face to exclaim, "What, done already?"

On Sunday evenings we used to be permitted to play, if we did not make much noise; now a mere titter is sufficient to send us into corners!

"You forget you have a master here," says the tyrant. "I'll demolish the first who puts me out of temper! I insist on perfect sobriety and silence. Oh, boy! was that you? Frances,

[119]

darling, pull his hair as you go by; I heard him snap his fingers."

Frances pulled his hair heartily; and then went and seated herself on her husband's knee, and there they were, like two babies, kissing and talking nonsense by the hour—foolish palaver that we should be ashamed of.

We made ourselves as snug as our means allowed in the arch of the dresser. I had just fastened our pinafores together, and hung them up for a curtain, when in comes Joseph, on an errand from the stables. He tears down my handiwork, boxes my ears, and croaks:

"T' maister nobbut just buried, and Sabbath nut oe'red, und t' sahnd uh't gospel still i' yer lugs, and yah darr be laiking! Shame on ye! Sit ye dahn, ill childer! They's good books eneugh if ye'll read 'em; sit ye dahn'n and think uh yer sowls!"

Saying this, he compelled us to square our positions that we might receive, from the far-off fire, a dull ray to show us the text of the lumber he thrust upon us.

I could not bear the employment. I took my dingy volume by the scroop and hurled it into the dog kennel, vowing I hated a good book.

Heathcliff kicked his to the same place.

Then there was a hubbub!

"Maister Hindley!" shouted our chaplain. "Maister, coom hither! Miss Cathy's riven th' back off *Th' Helmet uh Salvation*, un' Heathcliff's pawsed his fit intuh t' first part uh *T' Broad Way to Destruction!* It's fair flaysome ut yah, let 'em goa on this gait. Ech! th' owd man ud uh laced 'em properly—bud he's goan!"

Hindley hurried up from his paradise on the hearth, and seizing one of us by the collar, and the other by the arm, hurled both into the back kitchen, where, Joseph asseverated, "owd Nick" would fetch us as sure as we were living; and so, comforted, we each sought a separate nook to await his advent.

I reached this book, and a pot of ink from the shelf, and pushed the house door ajar to give me light, and I have got the time on with writing for twenty minutes; but my companion is impatient and proposes that we should appropriate the dairy woman's cloak, and have a scamper on the moors, under its shelter. A pleasant suggestion—and then, if the surly old man come in, he may believe his prophecy verified. We cannot be damper, or colder, in the rain than we are here.

How little did I dream that Hindley would ever make me cry so! My head aches, till I cannot keep it on the pillow; and still I can't give over. Poor Heathcliff! Hindley calls him a vagabond and swears he will reduce him to his right place.

NOVEMBER 22, 1777

A glorious day! So warm no wrap was needed. The last traces of snow had melted. In the air hung a softness that belied that imminence of winter. Not a cloud, not a wisp of white across the high azure sky. Overhead, except for the sharpened angle of the sun, it might have been August. But the nakedness of the timber trees and the somber colors of the meadows and heath—sorrel and sepia and dun and sable—distinct as they were in the unfiltered sunlight, indeed bespoke November. What a morning it would have been to cheat the season, to go romping across the dales with Heathcliff, to find the brightest, warmest spot on the moor, to lie without touching as our spirits went out of our bodies and suffused with the pure clear ether and thus with each other! That would be communion in truth.

Oh, the contrast between the beauty without and the misery within!

Hindley saw to it this morning that, dressed in Sunday black as befits our bereavement, the inner household went trekking down the valley into Gimmerton. There Joseph sheered off from the rest of our company and proceeded to the ugly chapel they call the Methodists' place on the far side of the village, where he would enjoy a three-hour service under the conduct of the ranting mechanic preacher, as was his wont. The rest of us progressed to the kirk. There, according to Hindley's command, first Heathcliff entered our pew, then Nelly, then I, then Frances, then Hindley himself, occupying the aisle seat, our father's place. Relegated to the status of servants though they might be, Nelly and Heathcliff had no choice but to attend service with the family. Hindley would never have dared interfere with Joseph's right to schism.

How "all occasions do inform against me!" For his text the pumpkin-faced, bald-pated rector had chosen the seventeenth verse of the fifty-ninth chapter of Isaiah:

> For he put on righteousness as a breastplate, and an helmet of salvation upon his head, and he put on garments of vengeance for clothing, and was clad with zeal as a cloke.

As the preacher droned on, corrupting the sense and the feeling of the prophet's utterance by blandly ignoring the military metaphor and the passion contained in "vengeance" and "zeal," and squeezing moralistic pap out of his glossing of "righteousness," "salvation," "clothing," and "cloke," I was forced to concede to myself that Joseph's spontaneous homilies, for all of their viciousness, self-servingness, and hypocrisy, contained more vigor. Besides, I recently had been compelled by the curate to read and be examined on a work of practical theology, "composed for the Christian youth of both sexes, by an eminent Scottish Divine" of the last century, which took as its title and chief trope *The Helmet of Salvation.* (Indeed, it is the very book two Sundays ago I threw into the dog kennel, with some damage to its binding, and later retrieved. In its blank pages and margins I have been scribbling this autumn's entries of my desultory journal.) As a consequence, I held myself to be so complete an authority upon that particular text that nothing the commonplace mind and prosaic tongue of the rector might devise and utter could edify or entertain me in the least.

Falling into an oppressive boredom, rendered almost insufferable by the reedy voice and the insipid manner of the speaker, I took up and opened the Bible Nelly had carried with her, laid it on the pew between us, and began leafing through the chronicles of the Old Testament for a lively narrative that might engage my attention. Stopping arbitrarily, I commenced reading in the thirteenth chapter of 2 Samuel. What infection I felt swirling in my soul and spreading to every vessel that carried blood into every extremity of my body as I read:

> And Amnon was so vexed, that he fell sick for his sister Tamar; for she was a virgin.

Repelled as I was by what I was reading, so horribly fascinated was my mind, so fervidly kindled my imagination that I could no more desist than I could stop breathing:

> . . . and he took hold of her and said unto her, Come lie with me, my sister . . . being stronger than she, he forced her and lay with her.

Because I was drowning in the shame and guilt these words sent me plunging into, I had to look up. I heaved for a breath, so weightily that Nelly turned from the pulpit to me with one of those glowers of motherly reproach I so despise, and foolish Frances tittered. Whereupon I lifted the Bible onto my lap and kept my finger pointing to the fifteenth verse. As a moth is drawn to the flame, my eyes darted back to the terrible story:

> Then Amnon hated her exceedingly, so that the hatred wherewith he hated her was greater than the love wherewith he had loved her. And Amnon said unto her, Arise, be gone.

I gasped. Nelly elbowed me sharply. Too intent upon the horrible significance of what I was reading was my spirit to prompt me to make the return offering it ordinarily would. Frances giggled like a child.

> Then he called his servant that ministered unto him, and said, Put now this woman out from me, and bolt the door after her.

Closing the Bible on my finger, I could not prevent myself

[123]

from leaning forward and glancing around Nelly at Heathcliff. To see his hair and eyes shining in the light that streamed irislike through the stained glass of the window he sat directly beneath—it depicted Christ and the woman of Samaria beside the well—made my heart leap like a frightened leveret. Then, as if a giant paw hovered over where it had landed, it trembled so that every nerve in my body rattled and shook. Frances tugged on the sleeve of my gown so insistently that I tore my eyes from Heathcliff's face and glared at her with anger. The force of my gaze caused her to flatten herself against the back of the pew so that I confronted my brother Hindley's threatening scowl. After staring at him sufficiently long and hard for him to be informed that I would not be cowed by his insolent looks nor truckle to the authority he was presuming to exercise, I bowed my head and closed my eyes.

This time someone taking me to be praying would not be altogether wrong. I was thanking the ministering spirit, whether angel above or demon below, that had enjoined me for the nonce not to impart to Heathcliff what had been revealed to me at the honey-colored headstone. Suddenly realizing that that stone, with its fateful inscription, stood in the kirkyard just beyond the wall through whose window the streaming sun bathed Heathcliff, I shivered. With all of the love in my heart and with all of the strength of my mind and my body I resolved that never would I let Heathcliff know.

Opening my eyes, I sent them back to the print lying in my lap.

> And she had a garment of divers colours upon her; for with such robes were the king's daughters that were virgins apparelled. Then his servant brought her out and bolted the door after her. And Tamar put ashes on her head and rent her garment of divers colours that was on her, and laid her hand on her head, and went on crying.

The rector was intoning his closing prayer. Never again, I vowed to myself, as softly I closed the Bible and let my lids cover my eyes once more, never again would I permit myself and Heathcliff to cleave in the flesh. Yet always, I swore to the

[124]

spirit within me, always would our beings be entwined. To manage such contradictory motions would be the business of my life. I had chosen Scylla.

As I raised my lids again and rose with the congregation to sing the recessional hymn, I compelled myself to look away from Heathcliff. For fear my eyes would dart toward him, as the needle of a compass when it is let go after being forcibly held toward the west swings relentlessly northward, I dared not permit myself to stare even straight ahead. Rather, I compelled my eyes to move to the right and to take in the elegantly dressed, silver-haired, bespectacled gentleman standing first on the other side of the aisle one pew forward of ours. Then I made myself regard his lady, her hair the color of wood-ash, fashionably drawn up and knotted behind, wearing a teal blue silk gown with a high lace collar. Proceeding inward along the row, I scanned the flaxen-haired girl, dressed in a silk frock of lilac, with sleeves short enough to reveal her thin white arms halfway above the elbow. I knew her to be my junior by a year or two. At last my eyes came to rest on her brother, taller but slighter than Heathcliff, standing beside her and holding the hymnal for her. All I could see of his face was his fair cheek and alabaster temple, over which a lock of light brown hair curled like a twist of honeysuckle vine.

The Linton children, Edgar and Isabella, the curate never tires of reminding Heathcliff and me, are well-bred, neat, respectfully obedient.

Their papa, I know, is very, very rich. They live in Thrushcross Grange, four miles across the moor where it dips toward the valley near Gimmerton.

So that my forehead might be bedaubed with ashes, I wished this day the first day of Lent, wished myself a papist. As for the crying, though I shed no tears and permitted no sobs to escape me, my soul wailed with misery, torment, and grief. Arriving home, after enduring Hindley's blustering warnings and threats, Frances's sniggling, and Nelly's reproaches for my misconduct during service, I went racing up to my chamber, tore open the press, in the bottom of which

[125]

lay the apron with that purple stain no amount of scouring and bleaching could remove, snatched the telltale garment, carried it with me into the oak cabinet, slid the panels closed behind me.

Seizing the strings of the apron, I wrapped them around my fists and flung my arms apart with such force that the strings pulled free from the skirt. Then I clasped bunches of the bulk of the apron in both hands and tried to rend the fabric. Jerk and fling and tug as I might, I could not make it tear. In fury I snatched the middle of the cloth with my teeth, clamped them on it, and pulling against what I held securely winched round my fists, I bobbed and twisted and shook my head like a dog gone mad. With a blood-chilling shiver the cloth ripped apart. I tore and tore and tore, until the shreds I made were too small to wrap round my fists. On my tongue I had the feel and the taste of linsey-woolsey.

My teeth still ache.

As I set down this entry in my journal, I'm waiting for Heathcliff. He, after being thrashed by Joseph in the wash-house—it seems that Hindley, coward that he is, is becoming chary of raising his own hand against Heathcliff—must gather the slops from the dinner table and feed them to the dogs and then must draw water from the pump sufficient for the house-hold for the next few days, after which he is to join me in the prison of our chamber, to which we have been banished for the remainder of the afternoon and for the evening until sup-per time. Hindley himself fastened the bolt on the outside of the door.

What provoked this chastisement? After we had finished dinner, Hindley compelled Heathcliff and me to join Frances and him in the sitting room. It is clear that when an opportu-nity for harrying offers itself, Heathcliff, instead of being dismissed as a servant according to Hindley's decree, is indeed kept within proximity. No sooner had we entered than Heath-cliff and I were instructed to edify ourselves either by meditat-ing on our sins in silence or by reading a devotional treatise of

[126]

Hindley's choosing. Meanwhile Hindley and Frances would do whatever they chose. Heathcliff and I elected silence.

Hindley's express intent, I have no doubt, was malicious. First he wished to intensify our suffering from the strictures imposed upon us by making us witness his and Frances' freedom—though were Heathcliff and I plunged into boiling pitch to our nostrils never for an instant could we envy those two calves. His second purpose was to offer us every opportunity, indeed to create conditions that would make it impossible for us not to violate his injunction, so that then a physical punishment might be visited upon us with seeming justice.

We watched and we listened to, or I should say we tried to ignore, their ogling and petting and pecking and mewling, for what seemed to be the duration of one of Joseph's sermons, which I should have preferred to have to thole. But came the instant when we could forbear no longer—Hindley's bait was too tempting. Of one accord Heathcliff and I, our eyes catching, let the slightest laugh of derision escape us.

Dropping the milk-white hand of Frances, which he had been licking as if it were a bowl of cream, he a kitten, Hindley sprang to his feet. We might have been Iago and Cassio, he Othello about to proclaim, "Look, if my gentle love be not rais'd up!"—so grandly did he roll his eyes from Heathcliff to me and back to Heathcliff, as he stood across from us, astride and akimbo. I had to divert into a muffled snort the guffaw that erupted within me at so ridiculous a transformation.

"Ah ha," roared Hindley, "laughing on the Sabbath!" Then turning to his mistress, who watched with a spiteful grin, "You see, Frances darling, how futile it is to expect a villainous gypsy and a disrespectful brat to behave like Christians. But," he added, shifting from a coo back to a screech and striding toward me as if he meant to snap me up in his beak and shake me silly, "I'll teach the little wench to mind her manners and know her duty."

Quick as a flash Heathcliff was on his feet, interposing himself between Hindley and me.

"Don't strike her," he snarled through his teeth, so fiercely

[127]

that Hindley stopped short. "She wasn't the one who laughed. I was."

"Why you accursed street arab!" Hindley gasped. Then steeling his voice with anger, he shouted, "How dare you interfere with my chastisement of my own foolish sister! I'll have you flogged for this insolence till your sooty hide is fit only for a tannery. Joseph! Joseph!"

Before either could strike a blow, Joseph, croaking he'd "flay t' yung divil 'n efterward slam t' boards i' his fayce," followed by Nelly, came stumping in from the kitchen. Almost grown as he is, Heathcliff is yet no match for the huge old man, who still possesses the strength of a draught horse. So, with lips mashed together, eyes glaring like a cornered animal's, Heathcliff was dragged off by the collar for a lacing in the wash-house. And I was exiled to my chamber, where I was no sooner secured than Nelly appeared with the further terms of our sentence. While waiting for Heathcliff to join me in prison, I have been writing this account of this another dreadful Sunday.

Banishment? Punishment? Prison? How can even Hindley be so stupid as to imagine that either Heathcliff or I considers removal from the company of his and his noddy of a bride a banishment? Whoever would consider being alone with Heathcliff a punishment? I'd gladly accept a thrashing from Joseph to be able to be with Heathcliff afterward. And whatever makes Hindley believe that when he chooses to send Nelly to draw back the bolt and release us from this "prison," whether it be before supper or not till evening prayers, Heathcliff and I, the "prisoners," will be here?

Heathcliff, I fear, will urge me to accompany him to Penistone Crags. That I must not do. Although he has acquiesced each time I have retreated from the look and the touch and the offering of himself which before that instant at the honey-colored headstone would commence our cleaving, I read perplexity in his face and carriage. The illness I am pleading, which my demon knows is real, not feigned, can serve as an excuse only for a limited time. To see Heathcliff beginning silently to question me when I could never deceive or mislead

[128]

or withhold from him save in the single instance that deter-
mines our mutual life and death is torture. Yet God and Satan
know that my illness is of heart and soul as well as of body.
How carefully I must hold myself with Heathcliff! For he is
more then perspicacious, more than clairvoyant where it
touches me; he senses, thinks, knows as I do because a part of
him and a part of me are one. I, realizing him as he realizes
me, perceive that he cherishes the notion that were we to
return to the place of our first cleaving and to the place
through the years we most often have returned, whatever the
inhibiting sickness, it would be healed.

Would that were possible! How I suffer at having to deny
Heathcliff what most I long to give! Yet Heathcliff reads me
accurately: so powerfully would Penistone, with all its affecting shapes and sounds and colors and lights, stir my soul, so
forcefully would it touch and move the deepest part of my
being, where hungrily I crave the cleaving, that much I fear I
should let myself and Heathcliff with me be swept to destruction down the swirling throat of Charybdis.

Young as I am, still I am a woman. That I know. As Heathcliff is a man. Although already we are wed, never can we
marry. Heathcliff must never learn why. Yet I must marry,
that also I know. Not merely because my father, negligent of
his affairs for many years, then stricken and disabled, at last
cut off in what I truly believe was his intention, failed to
provide for me. Not only because my petty and avaricious
brother so repels me that I cannot indefinitely continue under
his roof, beholden to him. Not just because without losing
Heathcliff, who is my life, I must interpose an insurmount-
able barrier between our bodies, must unconditionally deny
the longing we share to cleave our separate flesh. For all of
these reasons, and also because I must find a means to aid,
abet, promote, and at the same time retain, possess, and be
possessed by Heathcliff, I must marry.

Even though I am a woman, I cannot marry at twelve. Nor
at thirteen. But I must look ahead. In our wild and cut-off
region many a bride stands before the altar at fifteen or six-
teen. So remotely do we live that I shall not be able to meet

many men who possess the fortune I shall require to transform Heathcliff into a gentleman. And I am mindful that despite the antiquity of our blood and the respectability of the name Earnshaw, in the larger world, coming virtually empty-handed, I shall not be considered a very desirable prize. All that I possess—I say it without a trace of vanity—is a certain beauty, not the frail, the soft, the wanting to be fondled beauty of that clawless, milk-toothed kitten Frances. Not the doll-like beauty of the porcelain-skinned, flaxen-haired girl I saw across the aisle in the kirk at this morning's service. Rather mine is a spirited beauty, angular in its lines, irregular of proportion, imperfect in symmetry, changeable in its coloring, unpredictable in its mood, harsh in its expression, vigorous in its manner, wild and desperate and passionate at its core.

Conniving? For myself I scorn to bedizen myself, to ogle, flirt, tease, mince, playact, coquette, barter body and soul for a husband, be he gentleman, nobleman, marquis, duke, who enjoys the purse of Fortunatus, the wealth of Croesus. But for Heathcliff I would scheme to marry the pope and would drink the blood of the devil at the wedding.

When after his flogging, Heathcliff and I crawl out through the casement window within my oak cabinet bed and climb down the fir tree beside the house, I shall see that we turn our faces away from Penistone Crags, that we head toward Thrushcross Grange. By the amber light of the waxing moon, the bottom of which is full and heavy as the base of a ripe pear.

DECEMBER 26, 1777

When I persuaded Heathcliff to head toward Thrushcross Grange rather than Penistone Crags, I little thought I should not return to the Heights for a full month. Thirty-one days have I spent at the Grange, waiting for the mending of my ankle, which the Lintons' brute of a bulldog caught in his teeth and mangled as Heathcliff and I tried to run clear of the grounds after spying on Edgar and Isabella while they lay squabbling before the fire in their drawing room. Had not this accident, though not of my devising, served to further my scheme, the separation from Heathcliff would have proved unbearable. Even so, my heart has been in greater need of nursing than has my ankle.

So fierce is my determination to promote Heathcliff's chances in the world, in spite of the machinations of Hindley, that I have put the time to good use. Indeed, I have returned quite the young lady, something I must be if I am to succeed. Already I have observed signs of success. Mr. Linton has been charmed by me. Impelled by her solicitude over my hurt and my flagging spirits—of the actual cause of which she could form no notion—Mrs. Linton initially tended me with her own hands, then assumed a proprietary interest in me because of the way in which since my mother's demise my manners and dress and cultivation have been neglected. Taking me under her tutelage, she lavished correcting attention upon me. Mim Isabella served as my model, at first condescendingly, then in sisterly fashion, only to have my visit end with some poorly concealed resentment over my bidding fair to outshine and obscure her as a brilliant belle. But what caps the globe is that Edgar, whether he knows it or not, is helplessly in love with me.

Besides seizing the opportunity to reform myself in order to win the good will and affection of the Lintons, I have made two discoveries which, though they seem to relate only to words, bear significantly upon my relationship with Heathcliff. Both appear to rest upon mere coincidence yet are fraught with meaning. Both have affected me so profoundly, howbeit in different ways, that had I not been determined to present myself as winningly cheerful, after a first awful week of uncontrollably low spirits, even the Lintons, imperceptive as they are, would have taken note that I was nigh overwhelmed by conflicting emotions of gratification and despair, of joy and anxiety.

Mr. Linton's library, which is many times the size of my

[131]

father's and so much more diverse, contains all sorts of elementary works, poetry, biography, travels, romances, and sermons, a feast of edification and entertainment. It is kept behind locked glass doors, with a pair of globes standing before them, like two Roundhead sentinels. To this treasure house I was provided a key and given unlimited access. Shielders, at first taken aback at the sight of me dressed like a young lady and behaving properly in the Linton household, was nothing short of dumbstruck at the diligence I manifested in reading and study, which, I might add, was in no way feigned. Among Mr. Linton's books is a large volume entitled *The English Dictionarie: or, An Interpreter of English Words*. On the title page it reads: "Containing Useful Information Regarding Origins and Etymologies from Earlier Tongues, with Examples and Illustrations of Proper Usage out of Authorities Modern and Ancient, Including and Especially the Holy Scriptures." Into this work I burrowed.

One day not far into my convalescence, I was under a cloud of melancholy that was occasioned by my longing for Heathcliff. The recollection of our forever-ended cleaving being so vivid, truly I could see him in my mind's eye, could see not only his face but every detail of his flesh, and in my imagination actually I could feel him around me and within me. The state I was in prompted me to discover whether the word book contained the word "pizzle," which he had taught me. Just to think on that word started the softness and wetness in my innards.

To my surprise, for I had thought it only a barnyard term, the word was there. It was defined as "the penis of a bull, often used as an instrument for flogging, as Hakluyt *Principall Navigations, Voiages, and Discoveries of the English Nation*, 1599, 'The Boteswaine walked abaft the Maste, and his Mate afore the Maste, eche of them a bulls pissell dried in their handes.'" The word "penis," which I did not know, looked curiously familiar to me. Not being able to identify my acquaintance with it I turned over the pages of the dictionary to where it lay—to learn that a penis is "the male organ of copulation," copulation meaning "to couple sexually, as Pagitt 'Heresiogr.,'

[132]

1661, 'Marriage, which is a lawful copulation of a man and a woman.'" More properly, I concluded, Heathcliff's pizzle should be called a penis. I further concluded that, albeit unlawfully, Heathcliff and I had copulated.

As plunged into turmoil I thought on this discovery, staring at those five letters, suddenly I realized where I had met them before: PENIStone Crags! The place, with its great protruding slab of rock, its patch of moss, its lips and crevices, the chasm into which flowed the gurgling water from the force, the deep seemingly bottomless black pool—the very place was a monumental landscape replica of Heathcliff and me as we cleaved, Heathcliff the penis-stone, I the gorge. Removed physically from Heathcliff as I was, sitting alone in the drawing room of Thrushcross Grange, I seethed with an excitement generated by my discovery.

I had not yet finished with the business. The penis of a bull, according to what I had just read, was commonly used for flogging. Was that, I asked myself, the leather implement, thick, grained such a dark brown as to be black in streaks, its one end split into thongs, which once years before I had seen Joseph's huge hand and sinewy arm, tanned almost as dark and exercised as tough as the leather itself, wield so that the whangs bit into the flesh of Heathcliff's naked back—the instrument of punishment Heathcliff still regularly renewed his acquaintance with?

Remembering the flogging I had witnessed while secreted behind some sacks of grain—the old man with his white hair flying, muttering maledictions as he lashed, Heathcliff against the wall of the shed opposite me, where the sheep were shorn and washed, not a sound issuing from his pressed-together lips, struggling not to wince or shunt in anticipation of each whack, trying but unable to prevent his knees from buckling as the thongs landed and cut—sent my mind reeling backward in time. I writhed under every recollected stroke as if instantly it were biting into me, I felt the afterburn. How strange, I thought, that when my father, upon setting out on that fateful journey to Liverpool, had asked his children to name the present each wished him to bring, Hindley the boy should ask for

[133]

a fiddle and I the girl should ask for a whip! Again I could see my father in his greatcoat upon his return, bulging as if he were a woman carrying a child who had reached full term, again I could see the coat fly open and the pieces of Hindley's crushed fiddle come tumbling out, again I could see instead of the whip I was waiting for, the swart, black-haired, gleaming-eyed Heathcliff.

From there I thought of the pain that Heathcliff had engendered in my life: the sympathetic suffering I had undergone whenever Heathcliff had been punished; the jealousy I had suffered over my father's preference for him; the misery I experienced whenever we were separated and the longing that I endured until we were together again; the hurt I had experienced the first time he had pierced me; the shame and the guilt I had been writhing under since my horrible discovery at the honey-colored headstone of my oldest brother; the conflict I had been suffering, torn between my desire and a moral imperative; the anguish I was living and would have to live, knowing that never again could Heathcliff's and my flesh cleave.

All that pain which Heathcliff had brought me I accepted, indeed I embraced. For it was part of a joy so large and so deep that the hurt was subsumed as the turbulent white water at the foot of the falls disappears into the quiet blackness of the pool at the bottom of Penistone Crags. The pain necessarily was a current in the flow of my life. Heathcliff, the bringer of pain, was in truth my whip, my pizzle.

Agitated almost to distraction by my discoveries and recognitions as I was, I sent my frenzied fingers leafing through the dictionary for the word I had so come to love—"cleave," my ecstasy then, now my despair. The first explanation given was: "To cling, hold fast, adhere, as Genesis 2:24, 'Therefore shall a man leave his father and his mother, and shall cleave unto his wife: and they shall be one flesh.'" A thrill that solaced, lifting me for an instant above the low-hanging cloud of misery and despair within which I had been living, shot through my loins. No matter how it appeared to the world, no matter what of physical separateness lay ahead for us, Heath-

[134]

cliff and I were not only one spirit but one flesh, we were man and wife.

As I read on, the thrill dissipated, I sank once more into the thickest, darkest interior of the cloud. "Cleave: to split, hew asunder, divide as if by cutting, as Psalm 141:7, 'Our bones are scattered at the grave's mouth, as when one cutteth and cleaveth wood upon the earth.'" Driven to know the worst, if more there were, as though my destiny were contained in, yes were determined by certain words, I plunged ahead. "Cleaved or clove or cleft, akin to cliff." My heart and mind leaped together. The very name HEATHCLIFF contained us both! I, the SHAW, the thicket, a part of the heath that was CLEFT by him. At once we were joined inseparably, as the earth is one, and divided, as the moor is sundered at the gorge, as a river forks into branches, as the tree trunk separates into limbs.

What wholeness, what incompleteness! What fulfillment, what yearning! What peace, what conflict,! What joy, what anguish! What beatitude, what torment! Indeed the word spelled out our doom.

I was in delirium.

When three days ago I returned to the Heights, I rode womanishly on a pillion girthed upon a gentle, immaculately groomed black pony, with Robert, the Lintons' most trusty servant, in attendance. I, who by the time I was six, had been able to ride astride any horse in my father's stable. Mr. Linton had given me the pony for my own.

To be sure, my eyes were searching for Heathcliff long before I had ambled into the yard, but he was nowhere to be seen. As Frances and Hindley received me, Hindley handing me down from the little horse as if I were an invalid, they outdid each other with compliments and attention. That they too had in mind a joining of the Earnshaw and Linton names and thereby their estates—though for quite other reasons than had I—was clear to me. I found myself scarcely able to endure without laughing the blandishments that fell from Hindley's tongue. And the touch of Frances's lily hands, as she undid the feathered beaver I wore and arranged my curls, made me want to pinch her.

When I entered the sitting room Nelly, whom for the instant I was truly glad to see, appearing white as a baker from Christmas cooking, removed the riding habit I was wearing while keeping herself at such a distance from me, for fear of flouring the silk frock and white trousers I had on, that in order to peck her on the cheek I had to stretch out my neck like a goose. So infatuated had Mr. Linton become by me and so pleased by my reformation was his wife that as the time for my return home had approached, they had had all of this finery sent for me from B___ as a farewell present. Glad as was Isabella, whose clothing I had been wearing—for though younger than I and slighter, she is enough taller that all of her frocks fit me quite as well as they fit her—to see me out of her own things, she had not been able to prevent her envy and resentment over these gifts from showing. Edgar had acclaimed me as might a polished courtier were I a beauty of the court: "Lovely as your habit, my dear Catherine, it fails to do justice to your person." I fear I laughed aloud.

Unable longer to contain the desire that had been increasing by the day, then by the hour, recently by the minute, I directly asked for Heathcliff while I slipped off my gloves. Hindley, I realized, had taken note of my restless head and darting eyes and was standing expectant. Upon hearing my question, he turned toward the door to the back kitchen.

"Come out here, Heathcliff," he commanded loudly, sounding for all the world like Prospero bidding Caliban appear from his lair, "and wish *Miss* Catherine welcome, as have the other *servants*." For the emphasis he threw on "Miss" and "servants" I could have slapped him. Frances snickered.

As he emerged from the shed, Heathcliff was a blur to me. But his presence alone destroyed whatever resolution to be prudently restrained I had formed. Rushing forward, I threw my arms around him and kissed him over and over on the cheek. I could feel no more response from him than I would feel were I to embrace the honey-colored headstone. Indeed, were the day sunny, the stone would feel warmer than he.

Stepping back and seeing him in focus, I was shocked at his appearance. His face was begrimed almost to blackness; the scowl he wore, the pinching of his lips, the furrowing of his brow made him look like a convoluted thunderhead. So tangled and matted was his hair that it might be an animal's coat. From his mucky clothing emanated the reek of the cow barn. He refused to look at me.

Reproving him for his crossness, I sarcastically asked whether he had forgotten me. I confess I wanted to wound him, so bitterly disappointed was I by this homecoming which I had desired so long and on which I had counted so much.

Gratification glowed in Hindley's face. "Shake hands with the mistress, Heathcliff. One time that is allowed," he admonished.

Heathcliff would not lift an arm or an eye. Sensing that he was on the point of breaking away, I took him by the hand. As I gazed at his fingernails, edged with black, the ragged cuffs of his jerkin, his clogs, how I wished that my own hands now were less like Frances's and more like his, that I had on my gingham gown, that my feet, instead of being shod in burnished leather, were inside my old sabots. Heathcliff, I realized perfectly, felt deserted and betrayed.

Snatching his hand from mine, he went sheering off toward the kitchen door, threw it open as though he intended to rip it from its hinges, then banged it closed as if he were flinging back an oath or a curse.

"Be gone, you gyp," shouted Hindley after him, "and the Devil speed you."

It must have been almost the moment I set foot in the Heights that the wound Heathcliff had made in my cleft reopened and the issue of blood recommenced. I am sick in flesh and in spirit.

If my homecoming proved dismal, still worse lay in store. Retreating to my chamber in despair, in order to don the cursed napkin, what should I discover but that Heathcliff's belongings, including his trestle bed, had been removed? In a

[137]

rage I was able to contain only with the greatest exertion of my will, I accosted Hindley. He was obdurate, observing that Heathcliff at best was a gypsy bastard whom our father in a foolish act of charity had taken up from the streets of Liverpool, carried home and raised as a foundling. He apprised me that in his judgment and that of all the respectable families in the vicinage, to permit a vagabond to eat at the table with the household, to sit in the living room, to receive instructions from the curate suggested that my father had been moonstruck. That Heathcliff from his arrival at the Heights until the accident that had kept me at Thrushcross Grange had been installed in the sleeping chamber with me, notwithstanding that my oak cabinet made virtually a separate bedroom, constituted such a disgrace that he trembled lest the Lintons or any other decent people should discover the scandal from the servants. The disclosure abroad of such a stigma, he foresaw, would cause Mr. Linton to see to it that Edgar and Isabella suspended all relations with me.

Furthermore, he went on, all the waywardness, naughtiness, disrespect, slovenliness, and wildness which I had exhibited ever since Heathcliff's arrival at the Heights and which he and Frances fervently prayed the influence of the Lintons had caused me to lay behind, he blamed upon Heathcliff. As of the moment, he informed me, Heathcliff was forbidden to speak to me, except to reply as a servant. Finally, reminding me that Heathcliff's continuance at the Heights depended solely upon his, Hindley's, determination, recalling that he had been inclined to turn him away immediately after our father's death, pointing out that every day Heathcliff remained was probationary and contingent, he specified the terms for his staying: Heathcliff was to be retained as a hireling; he was to live exclusively with the servants; he was to perform hard labor out-of-doors under Joseph's authority and direction. Should these specifications be violated in the least even on one occasion, Heathcliff would be gone with a finger snap. Hindley illustrated this point directly beneath my nose. I could have bitten off his fingers, spit them into my hand, and thrust them down his throat.

Nelly provided confirmation that Heathcliff now ate with Joseph and her, now sat in the back kitchen, now slept in a spare room next to Joseph's in the second garret. Not once during my absence, she added, had the curate entered the house. To her mind, Heathcliff had been broken in spirit, like an oft-whipped hound.

Hindley and the Lintons, I had no doubt, had been in communication and were now in collusion to keep me apart from Heathcliff. Small chance they have of succeeding.

During the two days following I scarcely saw Heathcliff. Not only had the execution of Hindley's decree rendered so much as a glimpse of him difficult; clearly he was avoiding me. Once I did catch sight of him in the stable, currying the sleek coat of my new pony. How bereft I felt!

Yesterday, Christmas morning, as our diminished band of worshippers passed out the yard on our way to Gimmerton, I spied him at a distance returning from the moors in the direction of Penistone Crags. A thunderbolt of pain shot through me. I wondered how early he had commenced rambling, indeed whether he'd been out through the howe of the night, for the weather still was unseasonably mild.

In order to celebrate the holidays and not incidentally to maintain the Linton influence upon me and also to strengthen the ties between Edgar and me, Hindley had invited the young people from Thrushcross Grange to the Heights for a Christmas feast—roast goose, boiled beef, mashed potatoes, boiled turnips, preserved cucumbers, applesauce, tapioca pudding, spice cake, tarts, gingerbread, sugar candies, fruit. Others of the neighborhood were to join the party afterward for the singing of carols and glees, and drinking mulled wine and draughts of old October ale. In the evening there would be dancing.

To my surprise, as we gathered at the table, Heathcliff emerged from the kitchen. I was further astonished to see that he had tidied himself, had donned his Sunday clothes, which, though they had grown rather spare on him so that his wrists and ankles showed, were neat and clean. And he had washed his face and combed his hair. I suspected that he had even scrubbed his hands and pared his fingernails.

No sooner did he appear than Hindley leaped to his feet and shoved him back into the still open doorway, and calling him the son of a drab, rated him roundly, suggesting that he was slyly come in order to filch Christmas sweets and fruits. With a curse he bid him be gone.

Nelly, who happened to be in the dining room delivering food, offered to defend Heathcliff, as was her wont, but Hindley would have none of it. Eager to display his authority before the young Lintons and, I suppose, hoping that they would bear reports back to their parents of Heathcliff's reduced status and absolute separation from me, he went on to ridicule Heathcliff for his cleanly and kempt appearance, then threatened to pull his obviously combed hair. Heathcliff, mortification showing as fire in his dark face, was abjectly retreating when Edgar, in a manner so unwarranted as to be cowardly, added his mockery to Hindley's, declaring: "His locks are already so long I wonder his head doesn't ache. Why, his hair's like a colt's mane over his eyes."

Like a stallion at gallop Heathcliff burst back into the room. Standing in the middle of the richly set table was a willow-pattern tureen full of applesauce that Nelly had just brought in piping hot from the kitchen. Snatching the tureen, Heathcliff, his temper now completely unbridled, flung the applesauce full in the face of his taunter. Sauce dripped down Edgar's chin, onto the lace ruffles of his silk shirt. I was not sorry. Anger flared out of me so quickly that I verbally assaulted my suitor for his offensive remark.

So enraged was Hindley that without giving himself time to consider he rushed upon Heathcliff, collared him, and dragged him back into the kitchen. Over the larry of Isabella's whimpering, Frances's lamentations, and Edgar's howling, as Nelly tried to wipe him clean with a dishcloth, I could hear scuffling and pounding on the back stairs, then overhead. Whether Hindley again enlisted Joseph's aid or whether Heathcliff's spirit was in such a funk and Hindley's wrath so aroused that by himself Hindley dared to abuse Heathcliff I did not discover.

Later from Nelly I learned that Heathcliff was locked in the spare room, his new bedroom, in the second garret. Because of the height of the gable, there being no tree beside the only window in the room, escape was not so easy to accomplish as from my chamber.

So miserable was I that I scarcely could maintain appearances for the remainder of the holiday meal. Not a morsel of the bountiful feast Nelly had prepared could I consume. No sooner had the additional company, including a good-sized band from Gimmerton, arrived for singing and dancing than I took advantage of the crowd to go stealing off. When Frances, spying me, asked where I was heading, I told her that I found music sweetest when listening to it from the dark at the top of the stairs. In my assertion lay more than a grain of truth.

Proceeding down the upstairs hallway to the back bedroom, Hindley's old room, I peered through the window. Inside the cow barn I could see the flickering light of Joseph's lantern, which meant that he was still milking. Knowing him as I did, I much doubted that, his chores completed, he would set foot in the house this evening so long as the "divil's tunes" were being played and sung and danced to. Rather, I felt certain, denying himself hours of his precious sleep, he would go grizzling off to a neighboring farmhouse in order to sit up and read Scripture and pray and anathematize with another servant who belonged to the Wesleyan brotherhood.

Up the rough-hewn ladder and into the back garret I climbed. Because the staple and padlock, which Hindley had seen fit to have the door equipped with when he had first forced Heathcliff to occupy that miserable premise, now stood fastened, it was out of my power either to release Heathcliff or to enter his room. Hindley, alone, I assumed, held the key. I scratched on the door. Heathcliff made no reply. I rapped. Still no answer from within.

"Heathcliff," I called through the board, "will you come to the door so I can talk to you?" Silence. "Please, Heathcliff,

I'm wretched." I heard him move to the other side of the door. To realize that only the thickness of a wooden panel stood between us made me feel less melancholy than I had for days. In spite of the solidity of the barrier, I had a sense of his presence.

"Heathcliff," I continued, "I must be with you to talk to you. I'm going to climb out the skylight of the front garret, walk along the roof, and drop through the skylight of your room, if you'll unfasten it for me." Still he made no response. "Will you? I shan't proceed unless I know you'll let me in."

He growled an assent.

Within minutes I was with him. I refused to take time to change from the scarlet frock I was wearing. Leaving my satin slippers in the front garret, the slippers I was to have danced with Edgar in, I stole barefoot across the roof under a star-studded sky, in which a waning moon, the color of a bitten-into plum, hung low.

As if by mutual agreement we refrained from embracing. And when we sat on the edge of Heathcliff's cot, the little trestle bed that formerly had stood in my chamber, we positioned ourselves at opposite ends. A heavy smell of old grain filled the room, making it seem too small for all of its lumber, the shapes and bulk of which I could dimly see. Heathcliff's reason for wishing to avoid my touch was, I understood, that his feelings had been mortally offended. *My* resolution, holding to which was like staying on red-hot coals instead of plunging into cooling water, was entered upon for quite a different reason.

"Heathcliff," I began, after we had been sitting in silence for a time, "I'm sorry for what has happened. Truly I'm sorry." Although his white teeth gleamed, I was scarcely able to make out the shadowy features of his face in the darkness.

"I'll have none of your apologies," he snarled. I noticed that his voice had deepened since I had been gone from the Heights. For some reason that alarmed me.

"Please let me explain. I . . ."

"Nor explanations either."

To realize that never in this life could I reveal the truth to him and to know, as I did, that Heathcliff's nature was such that anything less than truth not only would fail to satisfy him but almost surely would cause him to increase the distance between us made me resolve to offer no partial accounting or feeble excuse but instead forthrightly to declare my unalterable affection for him.

"I left the party because without you I was miserable. I wanted only, I always want . . . ."

"No more nonsense, Cathy," he interrupted. "Such words are easy. They roll off every silly tongue. To me they mean nothing."

"What do you wish me to say then, Heathcliff?"

"I want you to tell me directly, will you help me to murder Hindley and pour his blood down the front stones of the house, then run off with me? In short, tell me whether you love me."

Inside me something terrible was happening. Never had I felt the force that drew me to Heathcliff more strongly. It was as if I were caught in a millrace during flood and all that kept me from being swept to destruction were my grip upon the handle of the winch that turns the sluice gate. Did I love Heathcliff? Did I love the moors, the golden rocks of Penistone Crags, the gill and the water splash and the falls, the pool in the gorge, the air that swept over the slade and across the swells? Did I love my own breath? Did I love my own life?

It was not the murdering of Hindley or the running away that stopped me. Although I had not the least doubt that, should I concur, Heathcliff would indeed kill my brother and his own unknown half brother and take me off with him, I also knew that I could talk him out of such an extremity. But when Heathcliff pronounced the word "love," I, having stood and understood before the honey-colored headstone of Heathcliff Earnshaw, our *dead* brother, shuddered. I felt my hands slipping from the handle they clung to in desperation. Should I acknowledge that love Heathcliff I did with all my soul and blood and breath despite what I knew, I would be swept into the boiling stream in a trice and carried to my destruction. That descent, I realized, would send Heathcliff, who now stood safely in ignorance on the bank, plunging after me, to his destruction as well. A word ought not have mattered when the reality existed altogether independent of what signified that reality. Yet my life and Heathcliff's hung on that word—"love."

"I . . . I have more kinship with you than with anyone else in the world. Even than with Hindley," I faltered. As the sounds issued from my lips, I became aware that my fingers were wrapped so tightly on the wooden rail of Heathcliff's trestle bed that they ached as if they would bleed. I relaxed them. They tingled with numbness.

Heathcliff sprang to his feet. Striding to the skylight window, he stood with his back to me, throwing his words, like pieces of rotten fruit he was discarding as he pawed his way through a full bin, over his shoulder.

"So, you've fallen in love with that puppy Edgar Linton. I'm delighted to discover it. If I hadn't, I'd have taken him in my teeth by the scruff of his neck and shaken the last breath from him. Unless his neck broke first. I assure you I wouldn't have to shed a drop of his milky blood. He'd die of fright before his ghost would have a chance to go sneaking out of him. But seeing he's your cosset, I'll not even ruffle his hair. Much joy may you have of your puling, whimpering pet. As for Hindley, one day I'll settle my score with him without your help."

Though his words cut me as I had seen and heard the thongs of Joseph's lash cut him, I knew that to protest, like trying to apologize or explain, was futile. Nothing short of the full and damning acknowledgment, "I love you, Heathcliff, as I love my life," would suffice. On the other hand, I also realized that to manage the impossible, to be with him and to have *his* soul and to give him *my* soul without our ever again cleaving our flesh, I would have to injure him still more, would have to hurt myself much more, would have to go on wounding and being wounded until our lives ended. Coward that I am, to destruction I chose pain for Heathcliff and myself.

Suddenly we heard footsteps climbing the ladder. I sprang to my feet, out of fear not for myself but for him. Heathcliff never stirred. A key was fumbled into the lock, metal jangled against metal, as, I felt certain, the lock was being removed from the staple. The door chirked open.

There stood Nelly like a witch-bride. I glanced toward Heathcliff. In the light of the candle Nelly poked into the room, guttering in the draughty atmosphere, my eye caught a glint beside Heathcliff's thigh. When Nelly entered and the flame steadied, I saw he was clutching the pearl-handled fruit knife we had hidden years ago in the hollow at the base of the guidepost. Its blade was sprung open.

Later that night, having cajoled Heathcliff into surrendering into my hand the fruitknife, I used the point of its blade to scratch CATHERINE HEATHCLIFF, beside CATHERINE EARNSHAW, in the paint on the window ledge within my cabinet bed.

The Broad Way to Destruction

JULY 30, 1780, AFTERNOON

More than two and a half years have passed since the horrible night that last occasioned my taking up my pen. My existence since the cleavage from Heathcliff—learning the hellish far side of the word "cleave" that afternoon at Thrushcross Grange had prepared me for what was to come—has been but half a life. It's been a time of waiting, floating, drifting down the gill, knowing the waterfall lies ahead, indeed hearing the crash, but being no more able to shift the course of my flowing than is water itself.

Meanwhile I have grown full womanly. Despite my girlish fears, both of my breasts have ripened so that amply and equally they swell the bodice I now wear. In my loins I have become as mossy as Nelly. While I am not buttressed by my hips in so substantial a way as she, the span of my waist is a couple of finger-lengths less than hers. Periodically, with less pain and abated symptoms, I put on the napkin. It took some months before I could believe Nelly.

At the Heights during these years, momentous events have taken place. Life has come and gone and foundered. I now have a bonny nephew, in whom, innocent as he is, I should delight. I have lost a silly-minded sister-in-law, for whom I ought feel pity, in that she was cut off in her spiritual nonage, fading out of existence, in this hard clime, without ever having come alive. And I have watched a brother, for whom I should feel affection, having lost a pretty pet of a mate, turn to the society of local derelicts as he daily drinks himself into irresponsibility, then into viciousness, at last into insensibility.

As surely as Hindley is gaming and spending away the estate our father left him, so he is deliberately wasting his life. Hating himself as he does, he is bent upon taking with him on the road to destruction all traces of his existence, including his own procreated flesh and blood. I have heard him drink to his own damnation; and I have witnessed his near killing of his son. Even the shock and mortification of having to behold the deadly enemy he persecutes preserve the life of his child cannot effectively alter my brother's course or arrest the speed of his progress along the pathway to perdition. I witnessed this chilling event only days ago: after Hindley, while in a stupor, had carried his son up the stairs and then had dropped him over the balustrade, Heathcliff, happening to stand below, thrust out his arms on instinct and caught the little body, thus preventing him from smashing his skull on the flags.

Such wanton and vicious conduct should make me weep tears of blood. Yet as I find no joy in my nephew, as I never mourn my sister-in-law, so I feel no compassion or remorse for my brother. I have eyes to see, a mind to know, nerves to feel, a heart to excite, for I still breathe, feed my flesh, rest at night, awaken in the morning. But my affective organs are stunned, as if frozen or paralyzed. Although tempests rage all around me, it's as though I'm the unmoving eye of the storm. Or as though I'm dreaming and know that what's happening is only a dream and say to my dreaming self, "Wake up, Catherine Earnshaw, wake up, so the real life can commence." Yet I am unable to rouse myself. What is more, I know the dream in which I see myself watching the living and the dying and the degradation of those around me will some day soon transform into a nightmare in which I myself will be the suffering actor. Yet I lack the will or the spirit to forestall it.

If I do not come awake, neither do I die. In truth, I do not will to die. Dreamlike as my existence is, Heathcliff still is part of it. Hindley's need to torment Heathcliff has become so great that now it overpowers even his cowardice and fear. Thus, he finds himself unable to turn Heathcliff away, as he previously had threatened and I had feared. Yet though Heathcliff remains at the Heights, his and my relationship has altered sadly. By compelling him to earn his bread and his cot by long hours of hard labor, Hindley has succeeded in keeping us apart most of the time.

My brother's persecution of Heathcliff is constant, at once great and petty, both physical and psychical. For his part, all that keeps Heathcliff here enduring, I well know, is my hold upon him. Were that to be removed, instantly would he be gone. While he abides, only my express injunction prevents him from killing Hindley—something he easily might accomplish, given his strength and sobriety against his adversary's debility and drunkenness. What is more, he might commit the deed with impunity. With Joseph and Nelly and me witness to the provocation, the close to murderous violence with which Hindley attacks Heathcliff again and again, should Heathcliff choose his moment for doing Hindley in, surely he would be immune from legal prosecution on the ground of self-defense.

What moves me to forbid Heathcliff to kill Hindley is not sisterly love. Nor is it my repect for human life. Some members of the race are better not being. It is not even the religious imperative of the Sixth Commandment. Rather, it is what was revealed to me in a flash that day at my dead brother's headstone in the kirkyard. Precisely the horrible knowledge that forced me to keep Heathcliff from additional fleshly cleaving with the sister he does not know he has, compels me to turn Heathcliff's hand from the throat of the brother he does not know is the persecutor he hates. How the story of Cain has haunted me!

Denied the opportunity to do what he yearns to with every drop of blood that courses in his veins, Heathcliff is sadly affected. The glint of his eyes has become fierce, that of a starving wolf in the dark. On his face is an expression of brutish sullenness. And I have noticed that he has formed the habit of drawing back his lips, while clenching his jaw, so that now his teeth reveal themselves almost constantly, as if he were a cannibal hungry to devour the flesh of his deadly enemy. Those teeth show white, almost translucent, like pieces of jagged quartz. The incisors are sharp as a dog's. I can tell that, difficult as it is for him not to avenge himself once and for all by choking the breath out of Hindley or slashing his throat, he is aware that Hindley's destruction of himself on the rock of Heathcliff is a still more terrible punishment than would be his murder. Horribly, this knowledge must serve as Heathcliff's sole gratification; thus he debases himself.

Compounding Heathcliff's frustration is the paradox of our relationship, our closeness yet distance. I am unable to forgo his company entirely. Whatever else I might do, periodically I have need to be in his presence, as even the saxifrage, growing in the cleft of a shaded cliffside, needs a modicum of exposure to sunlight and water, some few grains of soil in which to root and feed its life. Whenever Heathcliff can escape the heavy hand of Joseph and the two of us are able to evade the suspiciously watchful though bleary eye of Hindley, we have gone off onto the moors together. Frequently Nelly has aided and protected us, not out of any kindness to me, to be sure, for she and I have grown progressively more distant, barely maintaining a sullen coexistence, divided as we are by the exclusiveness of our claim on Heathcliff and by the clashing of our tempers. Rather she is moved solely by her affection for and loyalty to Heathcliff.

At first I tried to pass on to Heathcliff what I was learning from the curate, in order that he not sink into the stupified bestiality of our provincial farmhands. And for a period he made himself my pupil. How apt he was! for he's more natively intelligent than I, I'm certain. But after a space he wearied of his instruction, his prospects, as he foresaw them, providing no incentive, his hard labor dulling his faculties, his frustrated hatred and passion turning his energies and imagination ever more deeply inward.

I suspect, too, that gradually he came to identify books and learning with all that I was becoming apart from him. For it reached the point where not only would he decline to be lessoned, but he refused to listen to any mention of books, ridiculed me for my love of them, and, out of perverse anger, I suppose, deliberately adopted uncouth ways, affecting rude language and clownish pronunciation, allowing his dress to become slovenly, even dirty, putting aside all manners, all politeness, all considerateness, assuming a slouching, reptile-like gait. Oh, those days when Heathcliff moved across the moors as straight as the plumb line of Amos! What with Joseph's hypocrisy, Nelly's crossness, Hindley's devastation, Heathcliff's degradation, and my unsubstantiality, the Heights has become such a hole of demons that the rector himself declines to visit. Nor will he any longer send the curate, either as teacher or as pastor.

Beholding the transformation of Heathcliff has been like witnessing Lucifer corrupt into Satan. And I've had to watch with the knowledge that I bear responsibility in that I have withheld his hand from Hindley, in that I have set the adverse terms of our relationship, in that at any instant I might terminate his frustration and suffering and self-debasement if only I could mount the courage to steel my heart, tell him who he is, and bid him go. But selfish coward that I am, I cannot release him. Though it be but half, I must have what there is to my life. Though it be but to live a dream, I prefer that dream to waking without Heathcliff. Such an existence would be empty as oblivion.

Meanwhile I have permitted Edgar Linton to court me. To keep him and Heathcliff apart has been less difficult than I might have feared. For Edgar is more than uneasy in Heathcliff's presence; he has not only a distaste for him but a strong aversion to him. At the same time he is envious of him, even jealous, sensing that when I put him off, as sometimes I do, I am preferring Heathcliff to him. And he puzzles why I persist in spending time in the company of a ploughboy.

What is more, Edgar fears Heathcliff. It is not so much fright of Heathcliff physically, for he senses that so long as he remains my friend Heathcliff would never dare to lift a hand against him. Rather it is the force of Heathcliff that he quails before, a force he can feel as it pulls upon me, drawing the center of my being to itself, permitting only the outer woman to have to do with her socially acceptable suitor. So he avoids Heathcliff, preferring that I visit the Grange, taking pains to ascertain that Heathcliff is busy in a far field or has gone to Gimmerton or is digging lime in the pit beyond Penistone Crags, before he will consent to come to the Heights.

Our house being the inferno that it is, despite Hindley's sporadic efforts to make a respectable appearance so as not to discourage Edgar or to alert his parents to the truth, and despite the efforts of Nelly to maintain some semblance of sanity and order and to present at least a facade of decency, it is a measure of Edgar's affection for me, of his hope to rescue me from hell and the demons I share it with that he visits the Heights at all. And what with the self-abasement of Hindley and the resultant chaos being common gossip in the neighborhood, the wonder is that Mr. Linton has permitted his son to continue to come to the Heights or even has allowed the sister of such a debauched brother to frequent Thrushcross Grange, especially since she is visited and visits as daughter-in-law in prospect and as future mistress of the estate.

Edgar, I suppose, has convinced his father that I, being removed from the pernicious atmosphere of my home and falling under the Linton's benign influence, as happened years ago while I stayed at the Grange for the mending of my ankle, shall be remade into a lady and a model wife. So deadened are my moral sensibilities that though my head tells me I should take pity on poor Edgar and drive him off from the demon he is courting, for he is a decent young man, my heart refuses. So I allow the charade of courtship to go on apace.

In this affair no demand is placed upon me. No need for me to dissemble and pretend and cater in order for Mr. and Mrs. Linton to extend invitations, cordially to welcome me, and to show me the favor I know they are circumspect enough to reserve for the wife-to-be of their son. No need for me to indulge or flatter or becharm Isabella, whose jealousy of me was dissipated, as she came into her own womanhood and beauty, into expressions of admiration for me and of her desire for a sisterlike friendship. To be sure, no need for me to play the coquette or to affect a desire that wants to be satisfied or a passion that needs an object, for Edgar to care for me with all his limited capacity for affection and to want me with all the cool fancy he possesses. If I seem to play a double role, it is not that I am actively deceiving on either hand. Rather, I do what I must: allow myself to be with the Lintons in order to be made into what they want me to be, and see to it that I am with Heathcliff in order to nourish my life.

Had I been less passive, had it all not seemed predetermined, had I not been watching myself in this dream I have been living, I suppose I should have found the splitting of myself into two separate and different beings unendurable. But given the immovable necessity I have lived within, I have had to blunt my powers of distinction and discrimination, to put aside moral niceties, to dull my sensibilities and stun my feelings and benumb my affections. I have had to live the unconventional, the undesirable, the extraordinary, the preposterous, the grotesque.

While doing so, I have ignored the religiosity of Joseph; I have tolerated the dander of Nelly; I have brooked the depravity of Hindley; I have accepted the favor of the Lintons; I have permitted the wooing of Edgar; and I have held on to Heathcliff, keeping precisely and always an arm's length between us. Instead of acting, I have been acted upon; instead of doing, I have been done to; instead of choosing the course of my life, I have allowed myself to be carried toward the falls. Beneath which the black pool lies.

Edgar has asked me to marry him. Scarcely a surprising development. Of itself his offer produced no excitement in me. As tacit accomplice of a necessity I abhorred, I had long been a conspirator against myself. The "yes" I had prepared was my betrayer.

What has set me to resume this journal, after years of willless inactivity, is not Edgar's proposal and my acceptance. It is, rather, what I have felt stirring within me the past few days. After meandering through meadows and fields in a way that seemed timeless, I began to sense a quickening of the water, I felt sharp rocks, I heard the roar of the force at the edge of the gorge ahead.

I was fully expecting Edgar to make his offer today. During my last visit to the Grange, two days ago it was, the final bend in the stream was passed and I was on the straight course that leads to the run just before the falls. It was my birthday. After a festive dinner we assembled in the Lintons' splendid drawing room. As the conversation lagged, I noticed some significant noddings of the head among Mr. and Mrs. Linton and Edgar. Some preparation for what was to come, it was evident, had been made.

"My dear Catherine," Mrs. Linton began, "as proof of the delight we take in your company and as a token of the esteem with which we hold your character and as a pledge that we intend to pursue our friendship with ever-increasing warmth, we beg that you will receive from us this gift upon your birthday." How meticulously her words had been chosen!

Reaching onto the trivet table beside which she had seated herself, she picked up a gilt casket and handed it to me, as I stood close to her on one side of Edgar. So formally was the presentation made that I realized every detail had been planned: precisely at what juncture, where each person should be positioned, who should make the offering. Isabella was out of the question. For Edgar it would have been premature, even presumptuous. For Mr. Linton, too intimidating for me. Mrs. Linton could carry it off in a manner that exhibited the proper degree of intimacy. As I accepted the present from Mrs. Linton, I observed to myself that Edgar's hand had been modeled on his mother's: small-boned, the fingers thin and tapered, so white on top that fine blue veins showed prominently. I opened the casket.

Lying on the purple velvet was a handsome parure of cairngorm, the neck stone being fastened on a long delicately wrought chain of gold. I exclaimed with appropriate surprise and delight.

"These belonged to my mother, at one time a gift from my father," Mr. Linton advised me, thus discharging his weighty prearranged responsibility.

Making my response as carefully as the present had been chosen—diamonds would have been too lavish; this heirloom, with its history, perfectly communicated the significance of the offering—I kissed first Mrs. Linton on the forehead, then Mr. Linton, I embraced Isabella, and I shook hands with Edgar. The difference between his hand and Heathcliff's!

The proffering of this trial gift was managed with aforethought as well as discretion. A full day was allowed to elapse, in which period should I have any reservation about what was imminent I had ample opportunity to make it known, before Edgar's portentous visit to the Heights.

Of course I realized that, without my being consulted or even being advised, Edgar's father and my brother had been in correspondence and had settled matters between them. That Mr. Linton's generosity and Hindley's niggardliness dovetailed seemed a surety. Never have I asked my husband for any details. I confess that I did not like the Lintons the better for the deftness of their policy. Nor did Edgar's stature increase in my eyes because of the obviously passive role he permitted himself to be thrust into. For my part, had I not been acceding to it all, I should have felt like a sacrificial pawn. But I should have rebelled like a queen.

This morning I awoke in half darkness. Slanting across the yard and the near meadow came heavy rain. Driven by a vigorous wind from the north and the east, the drops looked needle-sharp. The sky, the gray of slate, lowered so as to obscure even the closest slope of the moor. When shortly after breakfast Robert from the Grange appeared at the door like a herald and presented a silver-edged note from Edgar, in which he requested permission to wait on me at the Heights in the early afternoon, I could have little doubt of his business. I returned my permission. Even though I had known how imminent it was, even when I realized it was but hours away, still I felt myself drifting, still I saw myself in a dream.

Shortly after dinner Hindley left the house. No sooner had he departed than Heathcliff entered the kitchen, where Nelly was tying a crimson sash behind my dress of white lawn.

"Are you going anywhere this afternoon, Cathy?" he asked.

[154]

That question, forcing me to realize the answer I must make, bit into me and shocked me awake. As I had not for many a month, I felt pain. On the instant I knew that I was no longer meandering through the meadow but now was heading for the falls.

Although I was perfectly aware of my suitor's intention, had I thought there a chance of Heathcliff's being free I should have put Edgar off, sending back word that I felt indisposed. I would have had no fear that Edgar's proposal would not duly be made the next day. But rain never before had excused Heathcliff from outside work. Now it was too late to prevent Edgar's coming. In order to compose myself, I answered noncommittally. Knifelike, Heathcliff went to the heart of the matter. Even as he was indicting me for my faithlessness to him and rating me for my betrayal of myself, I, aching from his lashing, heard the hoof clang of Edgar's mare on the flags outside.

His face shining with expectation, Edgar's person as he entered lit up the room, despite the gloom of the atmosphere. He was elegantly dressed in a coat of pale blue paduasoy, matching trousers, and a white shirt with a ruffled front, lace cuffs, and a broad collar, onto which his brown curls hung. For his part, Heathcliff's face embodied the storm that had begun the day; and his rough-spun drab doublet and breeches seemed a part of him, like an animal's shag or the bark of a hickory. The contrast between the two could not have been more marked. I could not help feeling ashamed that the man I was on the point of agreeing to marry should look so much like a manikin. The doll-like quality about *him* made *me* feel painfully alive.

For an instant the three of us stood—I seemingly between two rivals, compelled to choose or else, as in former times, content to let them decide the issue forcefully between them. Had the first been fully the case, how easy the choice! Had the second, the outcome should have been in doubt no longer than in a struggle between a wolf and a lamb. Of the three of us, only Edgar was uncertain, asking me whether he had arrived before I was expecting him. Heathcliff, as sensible that the issue had been predetermined as was I, dashed out through the door. In order to follow him with my eyes, I stepped to the window, remarking to Edgar about the weather. Outside, although the sky was still overcast, the gray had begun to lighten in the south and the driving rain had ceased. Heathcliff was already lost to sight.

As I dashed myself against the jagged rocks in the channel I was being swept along, I fretted. Now I wanted to have done with it. And I wished Edgar, with his lack of perception and scantness of spirit, to be out of my presence. Nelly, either because she was naturally thwartover or else because she saw an opportunity to retaliate for some hard words I had given her the evening before—surely Hindley, after I had showed him the cairngorm parure, had countermanded his standing order to have her chaperone Edgar and me—remained in the room, pretending to be at housework. When I roundly let her know it behooved her to withdraw, she muttered that she had to be "huswifely thrang." My suddenly unleashed feelings flowing scarcely under control, as they were, and her insolence provoking me, as it did, I could rein myself in no longer. Snatching from her hand the cloth with which she feigned to be dusting the pewter, earthenware, and china in the delfcase, I seized her arm as though to escort her to the kitchen and drove my nails into the heavy underflesh above her elbow. She set up a cry, as if she were stabbed in the heart, in order to expose me before Edgar. Not in humiliation on account of his presence but because my blood was up, I slapped her across the cheek, making certain that this time she hurt enough to justify an outcry.

"Why, you fly off like a Catherine wheel, miss!" she exclaimed. "That device might well be named for you, you vixen."

Hareton, my little nephew and Nelly's nursling, who was playing on the floor of the sitting room at the moment, seeing his foster mother attacked and made to cry, began himself to wail, "Bad Aunt Cathy, bad Aunt Cathy!" My control now being shattered, in order to silence the child I seized him by the arms and shook him till he trembled.

[156]

Aghast at such behavior in the woman he was on the point of asking to be his loving and obedient wife, Edgar, blanching to the color of white wax, attempted to restrain me. His imprudent underestimation of my passion earned him a potent box on the ear, a blow that quite probably deaved his brains. As Nelly snatched Hareton and retreated from the room, Edgar stood staring at me, open-mouthed as a cherub in a fountain, bug-eyed as a lady-clock. The ear that had received my fist flared red like powder to which a linstock has been held. His lower lip actually quivered from the offense to his delicate feelings, perhaps too from his inability to bear a blow without whimpering like a child.

All at once he walked over and removed his hat from the rack on which it hung. I prevented his leaving the house by speedily planting my hand on the latch of the front door. We exchanged words, he accusing, I not so much defending as attacking in return. My emotions being charged to the point at which I must do something violent, either I had to beat him again with my fist or to break myself apart in tears. Although scarce aware of what I was doing, I was restrained from the former by something deep within me.

From there it was only a matter of letting me cry myself out of my perverse and dangerous temper while he gallantly comforted and assured me. Then down on his knees before me he went. Taking the very tips of my fingers, he declared himself and asked for my consent in a voice that was thin as a July breeze. Upon hearing my acceptance he kissed my hands. The sun, which had dispersed the clouds, came streaming through the casement onto his head and face, making him look like the angel of annunciation in one of our old altar pieces. When he arose, he drew me gently toward him and kissed me on the cheek, then stepping back while holding my hands, placed his lips for an instant against mine.

Since his departure, as I feel myself rushing forward at a pace I cannot slow, on a course I cannot alter, I have been struggling to bring my emotions under control. Now, although I must inform Heathcliff without delay that I am to be married to Edgar Linton, I must do so in a manner that will

[157]

prevent what most I fear—his immediate separation of himself from the Heights. In order to keep him here, without my being able to tell him why I cannot marry him, I must let him know for a certainty that my union with Edgar will be a gentle shower that makes leaves and flowers shine and moistens shallow roots, after which the sun will smile and there may even be a rainbow, compared to my love for him, Heathcliff, which is a driving rain that pierces to the deepest roots of the greatest trees and in its plentitude nourishes the whole countryside, enpurpling the heather on the moors, greening the grass on the swales, the bent in the slades, the leaves on the trees, plumping the corn and the nuts and the pears, feeding the becks and the brooks, and filling the gill that rushes over the falls, crashes to foam, and swirls into the black pool at the bottom of the gorge at Penistone Crags. Not Edgar Linton nor the Lord God Himself, who divided the waters from the waters, and the waters which were under the firmament from the waters which were above the firmament, and the light from the darkness, and the day from the night, shall ever sunder Heathcliff and me.

I dare not trust myself to tell Heathcliff face to face the truth of my love for him and explain the necessity for my marrying Edgar Linton. Should I undertake to, I fear that despite all my resolution I would reveal to him the oneness of our blood. Nelly! I'll make her my conduit. I'll inform her that I have agreed to marry Edgar, tell her I cannot marry Heathcliff for a plausible reason, namely, Hindley's enmity toward him and degradation of him, and I'll confess to her my undying, ever-enduring devotion to Heathcliff compared to the affection I may hope to feel for my husband-to-be.

Whatever enters Nelly's ear must come out on her tongue. Close as she and Heathcliff have become since Hindley banished both of them from the sitting room, Heathcliff more than ever enjoys her confidence. For her, to be able to reveal to him what she believes I want to conceal from him, that is, that I'm marrying a man I do not unreservedly love, will in her eyes be to do me a disservice, an opportunity she'll scarcely forgo. For her, to be able to inform Heathcliff why I cannot marry him will be to injure me in his eyes. For her, to be able to reveal to him my unalterable love for him will be to make me seem foolish and pathetic and thus will be a mortification of me.

First, I must put court-plaster on the wound I gave her earlier today. I'll be humble, contrite, eager for her ear, anxious to confess to her, needful of her advice.

Now, using the point of the blade of the pearl-handled fruit knife, which I have not returned to the hollow at the base of the guidepost where the paths cross on the moor but have kept in the little black trunk with the curved lid in my room, I must carve CATHERINE LINTON, on the side of CATHERINE EARNSHAW away from CATHERINE HEATHCLIFF, in the paint on the window ledge within my cabinet bed.

As I pen these words and prepare to descend to the kitchen, I hear the din of water.

JULY 30, 1780, EVENING

He's gone.

As I entered the back kitchen, Nelly was rocking Hareton on her knee and crooning a song. Just before I sat down, facing her, in the closing dusk I caught a glimpse around the end of the settle of a tangle of black hair. The rest of the being to whom that shag belonged was hidden by the high back of the bench. Only the Cheviot ram and Heathcliff have heads crowned so thick and so black as that.

"Are you alone, Nelly?" I asked in a voice that made clear that I was suing for peace, as I dropped onto the settle.

"I am, miss," she replied, docking her words. To let me know that she cared not a whit for me she went on crooning to Hareton.

"Don't be cross," I pleaded. "Where's Heathcliff?"

[159]

"About his work in the stables, I suppose," she replied curtly, as if to ask, am I my brother's keeper? How apropos a thought!

Then for a certainty I concluded not only that Heathcliff was occupying the bench directly behind the settle but that I was not to know of his presence. Believing I had come to humble myself before her, to confess my temper, regret my violence, profess my contrition, beg her pardon, promise to mend my ways, Nelly was pleased to allow me to expose myself unknowingly to Heathcliff in a most contemptible and humiliating light. I smiled to myself. For my own reasons I was willing.

Heathcliff did not stir. I was not able even to hear him breathe. Perhaps he was dozing. What I would go on to say, I was certain, would make him attend. For thinking only to serve me an ill turn out of vengeance and jealousy, Nelly had played into my hand. She was making it possible for me to let Heathcliff hear from my tongue what I had to be certain he learned. And she was letting me do so without my having to confront him. At the same time she herself was serving as a presence to inhibit any temptation I might find myself coming under to betray what I knew I could not divulge without causing our mutual destruction.

After I ate my large portion of rue-pie and shifted the conversation to the actual matter at hand, Nelly served better than merely to listen. By acting not only as confessor but also as inquisitor, she seemingly drew out of me every drop that I had to spill. I even managed to justify for Heathcliff his eavesdropping by bringing Nelly to proclaim defiantly that she would not promise to keep the secrets of someone who constantly and cruelly queened it over her. My enjoining her to hold my confidence private was precisely what was needed to guarantee that she would not. While the conversation proceeded, I couldn't take my eyes off the almanac hanging on the wall near the window, on which Heathcliff had marked big black crosses that looked like the signatures of our analphabet hobnails on the dates of the evenings I had spent with Edgar and Isabella, dots on the dates of the evenings I had spent with him. The tally was decidedly not in his favor.

It was a harrowing time. Indeed, I felt as if a row of iron teeth had been dragged by plough horses back and forth across my prostrate soul. Hurt and exhausted as I was, when finished I lay preparing myself to bear whatever would be required the instant Heathcliff revealed he had been listening to my declaration. I heard not the rustle of an arm or a leg on the bench behind me.

While I waited, expectant, I took Hareton over onto my lap in order to divert myself and also to bring him to the belief that I was not a bad aunt and was sorry I had shaken him. My relieving the nurse of her charge also freed Nelly to prepare supper. The awful restlessness returned. That rushing and roaring within stirred and drove me. I could scarcely sit still. Yet I wanted Heathcliff to be the one to disclose his presence.

Finally crabbed Joseph came shambling in, demanding to be told where "that diviling Heathcliff" was.

"In the stables or else the barn, I have no doubt," Nelly lied, for my benefit keeping up the pretense that she and I had been alone during my catechism. "I'll call him. There's somewhat I have to say to him."

Throwing her shawl over her shoulders, for already clouds were gathering for a fresh storm, thunderheads this time, she went scurrying out.

She was gone, it seemed, for hours. I construed the length of time she spent trying to prove to me that Heathcliff had not overheard our supposed tête-à-tête to be a measure of her guilt.

"He doesn't answer," she reported to Joseph when finally she returned. Then leaning over me she whispered in my ear, "Catherine, I think you should know that Heathcliff, who was reclining on the bench behind the settle, heard you declare your intention to give yourself in marriage to Master Edgar Linton. When you began explaining to me that you could not marry Heathcliff now because of the way in which Hindley has succeeded in degrading him, I saw him get up and steal out the back door. That was the first I was aware he had been lying there concealed. I can find him nowhere about the place."

Thrusting Hareton onto the seat beside me, so suddenly that he broke into a wail, and leaping up, I wheeled, seized the carved top of the settle back, and stared down at the empty bench. Only to it had I made my profession of love.

I rushed out through the gate, which with its chain dangling was standing open, onto the moor. Without bonnet or shawl. Half running, stumbling in the near-darkness, I went skirring up the valley, past the dead tree trunk, past the stone guide-post, following the low way along the roaring gill, past the water splash and falls, into Penistone Chasm. Great crashes of thunder rattled through the gorge above the pounding of the water. In the blackness of the fairy cave my voice echoed, "Heathcliff, Heathcliff!"

By the time I had retraced my steps to the point in the path where the way veers off to the north and climbs the rise toward the top of the cliff, the wind had so increased that it caught my skirts and billowing them like sails half blew me up the steep track toward the crags. I kept gasping for breath. Just as I reached the rocks on top and as, to keep from being blown across them toward the edge like a moth, I went scrabbling on my hands and knees as far as the beginning of the great jut of stone, the sky cracked apart, making a huge jagged fissure of brightness, then quick as a wink it closed again into blackness. During the instant the fire that burns incessantly behind the night showed through the rent in the sky, the rocks of Penistone shone brighter than ever I had seen them in the most glorious summer sun. And all that I beheld in that brightness was the honey-colored stone.

Not until midnight did the rain come pouring out of the basalt sky. Although I had returned from the moors convinced that Heathcliff was not to be found there, I would not let Nelly persuade me to enter the house but stood outside the wall of the farmyard by the road. The white linen frock I had worn to accept Edgar's proposal was saturated with sweat, bedraggled from climbing over the rocks, gashed in a number of places from catches and falls. Somewhere I had lost the crimson sash. My throat was parched. Beneath my clothing my skin felt burning hot, my nerves within me seemed aflame. My flesh and bones ached as if I had been roundly and soundly beaten with a blackthorn cudgel. I felt my blood rushing through my veins like water in the gill. Suddenly, as if the heavens were whinstone at Horeb that Moses had cleft with his rod or as if I were standing beneath the precipice in Penistone Gorge, water gushed down on me, drenching my hair and my clothes in an instant, cooling my skin, dousing the flames of my nerves. Cravingly I drank in the fury of the storm.

A bolt of lightning leaped toward me from the sky, seeming to cut the darkness like the lash of a knout. Over the roar of the wind I heard a violent ripping and tearing, followed by a clap of thunder and a crash. One of the two main branches rising from the crotch of the great fir tree that towered over the northeast gable of the house had split off and, smashing against the chimney stack, had fallen heavily to the ground. Another flash of lightning revealed the destruction.

When something made me think how the lapwing, prince of moor birds, lures the would-be intruder away from its nest, I gave it up.

SEPTEMBER 15, 1780

I remember writing my journal by candlelight in my oak cabinet bed.

I remember after that returning to the kitchen and sitting before the fireplace.

I remember gazing at the sky through the narrow window. Sometime after midnight the storm moved off and the sky became twilit. The faint light in the west was still waning when dawn crept in from the east.

[163]

The sun came up blood red, I remember.

I remember that when he appeared for breakfast, Hindley, egged on by that Abaddon Joseph, drove me to my chamber, accusing me of having spent the night with Heathcliff in the barn and informing me that this time I might stake my life on his "sending that fiendish gypsy about his business."

I remember that, galled to the point of disgorging what little lay in my stomach—I had taken neither supper nor breakfast—which felt as if it had been burned with a caustic, I fell careening into the oak cabinet bed.

I remember that when I reached up and fumbled closed the panels, it was as though they were two honey-colored slabs of stone being dropped on me from above, closing me into the blackness.

I remember wanting with all my soul to unhasp and throw open the casement and fling myself out toward the moor.

And then I remember nothing for a long, long time.

Sometimes I lay in the loft of the barn. Sometimes I lay in the dimple of the slade. Sometimes I lay in the fairy cave under Penistone Crags. Sometimes I lay, gasping for breath, under the black water of the pool at the bottom of the gorge. I was always alone, wanting Heathcliff.

Now fire flamed inside me, as in the bush Moses saw burning on Horeb. Now a hellish wind blew over me so that I could not get myself warm. Often I burned and shivered together, fire within, wind without.

Once I felt my legs had grown together and my cloven feet and ankles were buried beneath the heath, entangled and held by roots. My belly had grown moss. So thick and stiffly corrugated had my skin become that when I struggled to move it would not yield. I felt my flesh gone grained and gnarled. Out of knotty eyes I stared at my coloring: mottled brown and black and gray. Weary as I was, I had to hold up my arms, one shoulder-high, one over my head. Long green needles grew out of them and out of my hands and fingers; I could feel them emanating and pointing.

All that was happening to me I knew clairvoyantly. I beheld

faces and heard voices and felt fingers. But the faces were beaked, the voices chirked and cawed and mewed, the fingers were clawed and taloned. When beaks pierced my side, sap instead of blood oozed from the holes. Only the top of my shadow swayed, because I was rooted at bottom. Then a savage wind whipped, bending me painfully. Lightning played around me, forks of it. A terror that I would be struck and burnt and split apart seized me. I tried to cry out but I had no voice, neither upper nor nether lips. From within, muffled by my skin, came inhuman creaks and groans. My needled arms and fingers screaked as they danced in fury.

Darkness fell. I was forever wanting—the birds to fly off, to be able to move, to be quenched within, warmed without, to breathe freely, to be out of the thickness in which I was held, to leave the imprisoning shade. I longed to be on the moor, running, I longed for Heathcliff.

Night would not go. The sun was stalled over the Caucasus.

When the first tinge of light showed, I realized I was parched. As if it were stretched from the far side of the gorge across to where I lay thirsting, a swarthy arm covered with dense black hair reached. In its hand was a glass. The hand put the glass to my lips. They cracked as I opened them to sip. So seared and swollen my wizen I scarce could swallow a trickle. What dribbled down my throat tasted tepid and salty.

After the arm withdrew, I felt a thousand imps running up and down inside my arms and legs. The pendulum of the eight-day clock, its bob, which for some reason was the iron used for weighing potatoes that years ago Hindley had hurled against Heathcliff's breast at close range, swung back and forth, beating against the inside of my head. Beneath me the rock was hard. Overwrought as I was, I dared not toss and turn for relief, I dared not stir. For I lay all the way out on the stone jutting over the gorge at Penistone Crags.

The panels of my oak cabinet bed stood open. Nelly's was

the first human face I saw. I turned away my head. How long I had slept!

Then I confronted Joseph's crabbed features and agate eye. So that I faced the wall beneath the casement window, I rolled onto my side. After the fever dream I felt cool and damp.

Next I beheld Hindley's face. Ghastly. Flinging myself onto my stomach, I buried my own face in the pillow and bit so hard my teeth ached. I tasted ticking and feathers.

When Mrs. Linton's countenance stared down at me, I stared back. Neither of us moved a muscle.

Kenneth's face was smiling at me. Bending, he kissed my forehead. "You've weathered it, lass," he said.

The night of the storm had passed.

I've just returned to the Heights from Thrushcross Grange. During the week I remained at the Grange, upon Mrs. Linton's insistence, I recuperated to the point at which I was well enough to read once again and made generous use of Mr. Linton's library. Today, despite the four-mile journey in the pony phaeton, I feel strong enough to write.

Outside the open casement beside my bed, through the filigree branches of the fir tree, still as the veins in stone this September afternoon, I see a soft blue sky. Not a cloud hangs or moves within the rectangle made by the window. When the gentlest of breezes wafts, as it fitfully does, I smell the sweet odor of hay the hands have been cutting in the near meadow.

But no one is working at this hour. Except for Sarah, the dairymaid, I have the house to myself. For the second time within the week Hindley has held himself sober enough to lead Nelly and Joseph and those of the hands who wished to go, all dressed in black, down the valley to the Gimmerton kirkyard. Today it is Edgar's father who is being laid in the ground. He'll rest beside Edgar's mother, on whose grave the rusted sods have not yet had time to reroot.

Mr. Linton took the fever from Mrs. Linton. There can be no doubt that Mrs. Linton, as a bitter return upon her kindness in visiting me here during the depths of my illness and upon her solicitude and generosity in removing me from this inferno to the well-ordered paradise of the Grange for the completion of my convalesence, received the fever from me. I came by it from the wind and the rain, as if they were a curse flung backward upon the whole house of Earnshaw.

Although I have not yet informed him of my resolution, I have decided not to marry Edgar Linton for three years. There must be a long time of mourning. And a term of waiting.

While meditating during my recuperation I have formed some other determinations. I shall be affectionate to Edgar and to Isabella. Through me they are orphaned, suffering grievous double loss within a very short space. I shall mold myself to the figure and discipline myself into the dignity befitting the future mistress of Thrushcross Grange. To occupy such a position, I quite realize, is no little honor. And I shall study to teach myself patience, forbearance, forgiveness, kindness, humility—virtues in which to this point of my life I have been culpably deficient.

Furthermore, I shall hold myself aloof from Hindley when he is rabid. I shall cherish my nephew Hareton. And as the first step in the new way I have chosen to follow, I shall try and better try to make myself something more than civil to Nelly, to whom, except as a servant, I have not uttered a word since recovering from my illness.

My reservation carries no provision for a change in my relationship with Joseph. To accede to his miscreance would be no exercise in atonement but an unconscionable capitulation of the spirit.

The Codicil

As I predetermined, this transcription, the full-fleshed experience, must never be perused by any other eye. An incarnation, it has served its purpose. Now it must go up in smoke.

My husband is a man of unexceptionable probity. To the letter will he execute this the codicil I am appending to my last will and testament. Not only will he himself, as I shall fittingly specify, put a brimstone match to these sheets without reading a word. Also he will honor without question a final curious provision I shall include, namely, that in the hope that at some future time a sympathetic eye might take the pains to decypher my faded hieroglyphics and make of them what it will, the bare bones of this journal be preserved.

Accordingly, I shall command my husband to return the four antique volumes in which the hand that at this moment is about to inscribe these final words, in earlier days left its little record, to the ledge of the oak cabinet bed in my old bedroom at Wuthering Heights.

Soon I am to leave this place, I know. As I sit here, pen in hand, having just mended a quill with a gold-handled penknife Edgar gave me as a present shortly after our wedding in Gimmerton kirk in April, at my desk within the window of the closet off my bedroom, smelling in the soft breeze the ripe odors of harvest, I feel as surely as yesterday I felt the little leap of life within my womb that something in me will split and my own life will go leaking out in crimson. Accepting my death as I do, I know because I will it that I shall not die before I have come to term.

Though in my few years I have seen too little of the smile of the sun, now I long for the dark. There will all of my earthly bonds be severed. There, where all are kin, will I and my bridegroom-brother cleave as once we did in childhood's love.

While I wait dressed in my bridal gown, inside the black nave of that church in the ground, for my lover to appear, I shall ache with restlessness, I know. Should the bridegroom tarry too long, I'll send my spirit up across the moor in the wind, I'll rattle his window, I'll allow him to feel my breath in the stir of the air. My presence will haunt him, calling. I'll appear in chasms of light.

So long as we abide, he in the upper world, I at the underground altar, both will feed on desire and dwell in a house of misery in the country of woe.

Neither bands of angels nor gangs of demons will be able finally to keep us from our wedding. No more than now they can rob us of the bliss we once innocently lived together.

Our new innocence will be won.

At dusk last evening Edgar and I were sitting in the upstairs parlor. Through the open window, I could see over the treetops of the park of the Grange all the way down Gimmerton Valley, past the chapel, where the mist gathering above the sough in the marshes hid the heights of the moor, behind which lies my old home. The water coursing in the beck, brimful from recent rain, as it follows the bend in the glen, sounded beneath the rustle of the oaks and birches and aspens. Edgar, his book on his lap, had laid back his head and closed his eyes.

Suddenly Nelly appeared like a wraith in the doorway.

"Shall I light the candles yet?" she asked.

"Not yet," I replied. "It's peaceful without the light."

She hesitated, turned as if to go, thought better of it, and crossing to the window seemingly to arrange the baby work I had laid beside me in a heap on the teapoy, leaned so close that I felt her lips brush the cairngorm locket pendent on my

[169]

breast. Then she whispered: "A person from Gimmerton wishes to see you, ma'am."

"What does he want?"

"I haven't questioned him."

Realizing it soon would be time to draw the curtains and feeling a breath of night wind as it carried the chimes of the bells from Gimmerton, I instructed Nelly to pull the cord on the drape, then to bring up tea while I was gone downstairs.

I descended the broad old staircase, on the landing of which hung full-length portraits of my late father-in-law and mother-in-law, crossed the polished oak-lined vestibule, and opened the door to the porch.

The instant I saw him, standing beside a basket of ripe pears, his eyes shining in the gloaming, his sharp white teeth gleaming as he curled back his lips into a smile that I knew was a wrench of pain, I felt that old quickening in the current of my blood.

When he whispered my name, I heard a sound like the rush of water, or the heave of the wind.

Thrushcross Grange
September 30, 1783

Glossary

ABADDON. "The angel of the bottomless pit" (See Revelation 9:11.)

APOLLYON. Another name for Abaddon, used by Bunyan in *The Pilgrim's Progress*

BAIRN. A child

BALL. To clog

BANTLING. An illegitimate child

BARMY. Silly

BARTON. A farmyard

BAYARD. A bay horse

BEAVER. A hat or bonnet

BECK. A brook

BENT. Tall grass

BERLIN WOOL. A fine dyed wool used for tapestry

BESOM. Broom, the plant and the implement made of the broom plant that is used for sweeping

BEVER. A small repast between meals

BILLIE. A companion

BLACK. Black-haired, dark-complexioned (also used as a substantive)

BONNY. Beautiful, fine; also, fair-complexioned (also used as a substantive)

BOOTJACK. A contrivance for pulling off boots

BOURNE. A small stream

BOX. Boxwood

BUCKING BASKET. A wash bucket

BYRE. A cow barn

CAIRNGORM. A yellow or wine-colored precious stone

CANNY. Clever, cunning

CANT. Lively, merry; also to talk affectedly or hyprocritically

CANTLET. A small portion

CAROL. A happy song, often sung to a dance tune

CATHERINE WHEEL. A firework that rotates while burning

CHAPEL. A Nonconformist (Methodist, Baptist) church

CHEMISETTE. A bodice, often made of lace

CHEVIOT RAM. A ram from the Cheviot mountains. Cheviot
sheep are noted from their thickset wool.

CHIRK. To grate or creak

CHIVVY. To chase, hunt, pursue

CHRISTMAS BOX. A present or gratuity given at Christmas

CLAPBREAD. Oatmeal cake, rolled thin and baked hard

CLAP-NET. A fowler's net that can be suddenly shut by pulling
a string

CLEMMED. Starved, wasted with hunger

CLOSET. A small room off a bedroom, for privacy, often used
for writing

CLOUGH. A steep-sided valley, a ravine

CLYSTER. An enema

COLLOP. A piece of flesh

COOMBE. A hollow, crescent, or valley in the side of a hill

CORN. Cereal grain

COSSET. A pet

COTE. A shed or outbuilding for sheltering animals

COURT-PLASTER. Sticking plaster used to cover cuts or wounds

CRAUNCH. To speak with a crunching sound, as if grinding the teeth

CROFT. A small enclosed field

CULM. A stem or stalk, usually hollow and jointed

CUMBER. Trouble, distress, oppression; also to trouble, distress, perplex

CURTAL. Shortened, abridged

CUSHAT. A wood-pigeon or ring-dove

DEAN. To deafen

DEAVE. To bang, stun, stupify

DELF. Glazed earthenware made at Delft, Holland

DELVER. A digger

DEN. A hollow in the landscape

DOCK. A coarse weedy wildplant (genus *Rumex*); also to cut short, cut off

DOMINIE. A schoolmaster

DOUBLET. A close-fitting man's jacket

DOUBT. To fear, be afraid

DRAB. A slattern or harlot

DRABBLE-TAILED. Slatternly

DRAUGHT. A potion, a dose of liquid medicine

DRAY. To pull or draw on a cart

DRUGGET. Coarse woollen stuff used for floor coverings

DUNDERPATE. A blockhead, numbskull

EIGHT-DAY CLOCK. A clock that runs for eight days without winding, usually a tall clock

FESS. Smart, attractive, clever

FETTLE. To tidy

FLAG. Flagstone

FLAYSOME. Frightful, awful

FLUMMERY. Literally a sweet dish made of eggs, flour, milk; metaphorically nonsense, drivel

FORB. Weed other than grass

FORCE. A waterfall or cascade

FOREIGN. Coming from another district, not native to the region

FRAME. To go quickly, hurry off

FULLER'S EARTH. A clayish substance used in a cleansing cloth

GAITER. A covering of cloth or leather for the ankle or lower leg

GANG. A way, road, path

GILL. A narrow stream running through a cleft or ravine

GLEE. An unaccompanied song for three or more voices

GLEG-EYED. Sharp-eyed

GLOAMING. Twilight, dusk

GOWPEN. A double handful

GREASEHORN. A flatterer or sycophant

GREAT-CHAIR. A large armchair

GRIZZLE. To sulk, fret

GUTTER. To flicker in a draft

GYP. Short for gypsy; also a servant in a college at Cambridge

HAW. A hawthorn berry

HESSIANS. High boots with tassels in front at the top

HIE. To hasten, betake oneself quickly

HODDEN. Coarse woolen cloth

HODGE. A rustic

HOLM. Flat low-lying ground near a stream or river

HORNBOOK. A primer

HOWE. The depth or middle

HUSWIFELY. In the manner of a good housewife

IRID. The iris of the eye
IRIS. A rainbow

JERKIN. A close-fitting jacket or short coat
JOINER. A worker in wood
JUPE. A loose-fitting jacket

KIRK. A church, here the established church of the parish
KNOCKED UP. Tired out, exhausted
KNOT-GRASS. A common weed, coarse and tough
KNOUT. A whip used for flogging criminals

LADY-CLOCK. A kind of beetle
LARRY. Confusion, excitement
LAWN. A fine sheer linen
LEA. Pasture land
LEAD-EATER. An India rubber eraser
LEVERET. A young hare
LEVITE. A clergyman
LING. Common heather
LINSEY-WOOLSEY. A coarse wool fabric
LINSTOCK. A staff with a forked head to hold a lighted match
LIST. A cloth of heavy thread
LOPPY. Limp
LUMBER. As an adjective, timber or wood fit for construction, as in the phrase *a lumber tree;* also useless stuff, odds and ends; also to move heavily or clumsily

MECHANIC. Having a manual occupation
MEGRIM. A sick headache, often with vertigo
MERINO. A fine woolen yarn, from the Merino sheep

[175]

MEWL. To mew like a cat or to whine like a baby

MIM. Primly silent, demure, genteel

MISS NANCY. An effeminate man

MOHOCK. A Mohawk Indian

MOIDER. To perplex, bewilder, confuse

MOOL. A clod of earth, mould

MOURNING RING. A ring worn as a memorial of a deceased person

MUCKYMUCKED. Muddy, filthy, dirty

NAB. A projecting or raised part of a hill

NEGUS. A mixture of wine and hot water, sweetened and flavored

NODDY. A simpleton, noodle

OCTOBER ALE. A traditional Yorkshire ale, so named because it was brewed in the fall, often drunk at Christmas

OFFALD. Worthless, wicked, awful

PADUASOY. Silk

PARIAN. Fine marble, from Paros, Greece

PARURE. A set of jewels or ornaments

PATTEN. A sandal or clog

PAWKY. Artful, shrewd

PILLION. A woman's light saddle

PINCHBECK. Spurious or of small value

PINK. The most perfect condition or degree of something

PLAIN. To complain, lament

PLAT. A patch

PLISKY. Mischievous, tricky

POPPET. A doll or puppet

PORRIWIGGLE. A polliwog, tadpole

PRESS. A large cabinet or cupboard for holding clothes

PROOF. A test

PUIR. Poor (with a pun on pure)

PUMMY-SMOOTH. Rubbed smooth with pumice

PURSY. Shortwinded

RANNY. Wild, boisterous

RINDLE. A small watercourse

RUE-PIE. "Pie" made of regret

SABOT. A wooden shoe, clog

SAE. So

SAGO. A starch prepared from the pith of the sago palm tree by boiling it in milk or water

SAWNEY. Foolish, wheedling

SCONE. A round cake baked on a griddle

SCREE. A mass of pebbles, stones, debris

SCREED. An edging, a bordering strip or frill

SCROOP. The spine of a book; also to make a strident, grating, or creaking sound; also such a sound

SECOND SIGHT. Clairvoyance

SETTLE. A wooden bench with arms, a high solid back, and an enclosed foundation that is often a chest

SHAW. A thicket, a strip of undergrowth

SHOVEL HAT. A shallow-crowned hat with a wide brim curved up at the sides, worn by clergymen

SIEGE. A seat occupied by a person of rank

SKIFT. To run, go quickly

SKIRR. To run hastily away

SLADE. An open space, a greensward

SLUTHER. To walk with a heavy shuffling gait

SMALL-CLOTHES. Breeches

[177]

SOUGH. A bog or water channel; also to make a moaning or sighing sound

SPICE. A trace or touch

SPINNEY. A copse, small wood

SPLASH. A water-splash, that is, a ford or shallow stream crossing a path

SPOONISH. Foolish

SPRAT. A young or insignificant person

SPRINGE. A snare for catching birds, especially woodcocks

STAVE. A stanza of a song

STREET ARAB. A homeless vagrant child

SURTOUT. A man's long close-fitting overcoat

SWALE. A hollow or depression in the land

SWELL. An upland or eminence that is broad, smooth, rounded

TEAPOY. A small table or stand with three legs

TETCHILY. Peevishly, short-temperedly

THIBLE. A stick or spatula for stirring in a cooking pot

THOLE. To endure, undergo, be exposed to

THRANG. Busy

THREAP. To scold, chide, blame, rebuke

THWARTOVER. Contrary, perverse, self-willed

TILLAGE. The act or operation of farming, agriculture

TREACLE. Sugary syrup, molasses

TRESTLE BED. A portable bed supported upon trestles

TRIVET. Three-footed

VAMP. To make one's way on foot

WABBLE. To wobble, move unsteadily

WAIN. A large farm wagon or cart

WAMBLE. To stagger, move unsteadily

WASH-HOUSE. An outbuilding used for washing clothes

WATER-SPLASH. A ford or shallow stream crossing a path

WHEY. The watery part of milk that remains after separation of the curd by coagulation

WHINSTONE. Very hard dark-colored rock, such as basalt

WISHT. To be quiet

WIZEN. The windpipe or throat

WOLD. A tract of open country, moorland

WORK. Sewing, knitting, needlework

WORRIT. To worry, distress

WRITING-DESK. A portable writing-case or box that opens to form a desk or surface for writing.